English shipowning during the industrial revolution

FOR GEORGIA

English shipowning during the industrial revolution

Michael Henley and Son, London shipowners,
1770–1830

SIMON P. VILLE

Manchester University Press

Copyright © Simon P. Ville 1987

Published by Manchester University Press,
Oxford Road, Manchester, M13 9PL, UK
27 South Main Street, Wolfeboro, NH 03894–2069, USA

British Library cataloguing in publication data

Ville, Simon P.
  English shipowning during the industrial
  revolution: Michael Henley and Son, London
  shipowners, 1770–1830.
  1. Michael Henley and Son – History
  I. Title
  387.5′ 09421   HE9545.M4/

Library of Congress cataloging in publication data applied for

ISBN 0 7190 1714 9 *hardback*

Typeset in Great Britain
by Williams Graphics, Abergele, North Wales

Printed and bound in Great Britain by
Robert Hartnoll (1985) Ltd., Bodmin, Cornwall

CONTENTS

TABLES AND APPENDICES

ILLUSTRATIONS

PREFACE

This book, and the Ph.D. thesis from which it was drawn, arose out of the discovery of an enormous and remarkable collection of shipowning papers in the attic of Waterperry House in Oxfordshire in the early 1970s. These papers contained the story of shipowners Michael Henley and Son and had lain untouched (except for the attention of a few hungry mice!) in the attic of their house for nearly a century and a half since the demise of the business in early 1831. In 1972 the Henley collection was presented to the National Maritime Museum by Captain J. A. C. Henley, R.N. The business papers had been carefully sorted and filed into 116 wooden boxes during the firm's existence. They have now been catalogued by the museum with the call mark, 'HNL'. It soon became clear that the collection was an unrivalled source for the study of English shipowning in the formative half century after 1775, as well as offering a much greater insight into the development of the shipping industry in a period about which so little is known. In essence the papers offer a virtual day to day view of the operations of an early shipowner over the course of half a century, producing evidence on a range of issues from the rise of the business, the vessels they owned, where they sent them, the profits they earned to the firm's decline. The wealth of statistical information tells us much about industry wide trends in freight rates, prices and profits and is ably complemented by the large amount of literary evidence contained in surviving correspondence.

Between 1979 and 1984 I wrote a Ph.D. at London University ('Michael Henley and Son, London shipowners, 1775–1830; with special reference to the war experience') which used the Henley experience to demonstrate the critical impact that the wartime economy had on the development of shipping and shipowning. Since 1979 the growth of individual business histories made it clear that a study of Henley's in their own right, rather than as

an indicator of a particular economic effect, was needed; such is
the intention of this work. The book is unique in its field; there
is no other study of an individual shipowner during this critical
period which witnesses the emergence of the professional shipowner and the beginnings of England's 'industrial revolution'.
As well as explaining the Henley experience and fitting it within
the context of English shipowning, I have used the material,
supplemented by other sources, to explore the development of
the shipping industry and its role in Britain's industrialisation;
areas which, again, are untouched by existing historiography.

In studying Henley's I owe an enormous debt to Mr Robin
Craig, who initially pointed me in the direction of the Henley
archive and then supervised my Ph.D., offering constant advice
and encouragement. I should also like to thank Dr Gordon
Jackson, who served as a thorough and tireless external examiner
and, more recently, kindly read through all the chapters of my
manuscript, offering many helpful comments in the process. The
National Maritime Museum, London were kind enough to allow
me to work on the Henley Collection while it was still being
catalogued. I am particularly grateful to Mrs Ann Currie, who
catalogued the collection, and Dr Roger Knight, the then Director
of Manuscripts, for their help and co-operation, together with all
the staff of the museum's reading room. My thanks also to the
museum (plates 2–6), to the Guildhall Library, City of London
(plate 1) and Mr Nicholas Ville (plate 7) for allowing me to
reproduce the prints. Mrs Susan Spence was kind enough to type
several drafts of the book and Georgia Searle read the proofs.
Finally, I would also like to express my gratitude to the trustees
of the Twenty-seven Foundation at the University of London for
a grant which financed the final stages of the preparation of this
manuscript.

S.V.

University of Manchester Institute of Science and Technology

1 · The growth of the professional shipowner

Traditionally, investors in shipping were drawn from a wide social and geographical spread of the population, people from many walks of life, including widows, gentlemen, farmers and colliery owners.[1] In the eighteenth century there were few outlets for the small investor; most modern financial institutions did not exist, whilst industrial investment was curtailed by the 'Bubble' Act of 1719[2] and the desire of most entrepreneurs to maintain control and ownership of the enterprise. Shipping was therefore exceptional and suitable for the small investor because of the relatively low share denominations. For the purpose of ownership, vessels were usually divided into sixty-four shares that were completely independent pieces of property. Share owners were regarded as 'tenants-in-common', leaving them free to buy and sell their shares without reference to other owners. Most investors were passive, leaving the running of the venture, to the master or a managing owner. An investor would not have to own a whole ship but could buy as little as one sixty-fourth share. Since many vessels were old, this kept down the size of the investment. The absence of effective marine insurance at the beginning of the eighteenth century encouraged shared ownership as people took care to spread risks, 'a quarter of four ships was undoubtedly a better investment than the whole of one'.[3]

Partnerships were the main form of business structure but they were not without problems. Lack of limited liability discouraged sleeping partners from investing, whilst new partners could not be admitted without the consent of all the others. The shipping industry was different from this, being governed by Admiralty law which was centred not on the person but on the ship. The effect was to create a corporation based on each vessel. By this means there was a degree of limited liability and shares were freely transferable by the use of a bill of sale. Moreover, the Registration Act of 1786[4] gave some protection to investors by recording the names, addresses and occupations of owners and giving particulars identifying the vessel.

The majority of investors were, nonetheless, already associated with the shipping and mercantile trades. An anonymous writer noted that, 'almost every tradesmen whose business was connected with shipping employed some part of his property in that line to extend his business'.[5] Merchants realised that the ownership of a few vessels could serve as a useful adjunct to their business, offering, for example, the market security of vertical integration. This was especially so in the coal trade where many merchants and colliery owners invested in shipping. In ancillary trades of shipping, mastmakers and ship chandlers bought shares in order to extend their business patronage and because of their specialist knowledge of the field.

It was not until the later eighteenth century that shipowning emerged as a distinct and specialist occupation on a large scale. Professional owners, concentrating most or all of their capital and enterprise on shipping, began to emerge. For them, shipowning was no longer to be regarded as an adjunct of another business. Interestingly, the term 'shipowner' does not appear in the directories of Bristol, Liverpool or Newcastle in the eighteenth century, nor that of London until 1815.[6] As the eighteenth century developed, there was a trend towards fewer owners, on average, of a vessel and the frequent emergence of a single majority shareholder who acted as manager in return for a commission as well as his share of the profits. This was the first tentative step towards the 'concentration of ownership and professionalisation of management which were to lead ... to the separation and specialisation of merchant and shipowner'.[7] Clearly, this had much to do with the huge expansion of English commerce, fostered by the rise of the commercial coffee houses, during the 'Industrial Revolution', which permitted and encouraged specialisation and differentiation of function.

The increasing provision of marine insurance meant owners no longer had to spread their risks amongst many vessels.[8] Those who wanted a reliable and stable income would still invest widely in the knowledge that even when vessels were not lost, their profits varied considerably. Instead, it encouraged the dynamic entrepreneur who would be more willing to chance his capital in the hope of high returns. The wars of the later eighteenth century encouraged specialist owners. High wartime profits, from increased freight rates, attracted entrants into the industry and caused one contemporary to note, 'almost every person (who could procure the means) became concerned in shipping till their harbours were crowded with vessels'.[9] The risks were very great although, 'the losses served to increase the ardour with which they ventured their property on the sea'.[10] Nonetheless, the survivors in this high risk industry were likely to be men who already had some knowledge of maritime affairs and knew that if they were prepared to devote all their efforts to shipping, the rewards might be very high. Other owners, with less expertise, struggled against the problems of high shipping costs and manpower shortages.

The great demand for transports which led to the formation of the Transport Board in 1794, encouraged men to act solely as shipowners and not merchants. Frequently, transports remained many years in service and so owners became accustomed to only shipping and not merchanting a commodity. Compensation for the capture of transports removed some of the problems of marine insurance. Having a vessel in the service for long periods required little day to day effort from the owner, leaving him free to break into other trades which were higher risk in nature and required more work. This is exactly what was happening with the expansion of the Atlantic trades. Another possibility for the enterprising owner in wartime was the acquisition of prizes as cheap vessels. Prizes could make good and suitable merchant vessels and the fact that many were sold in London was clearly of benefit to local owners. The acquisition of cheap transports, privateers and armed ships at the end of the American War of Independence explains the development of many shipowners in the whaling trade.[11]

Most pioneer shipowners probably came from the mercantile and related classes; men who had some knowledge of the shipping industry and possibly already owned a few ships as an extension of their business. Small private businessmen would be adaptable enough to move from one line of enterprise to another as the markets fluctuated. Firms like the Rathbones of Liverpool or the Thomsons of Leith began as merchants. In Hull many shipowners had previously been master mariners or shipbuilders.[12] Alternatively, some shipowners were originally shipbrokers.[13] Far more research is required on the shipping registers before the occupational origins of most specialists can be ascertained.

How widespread were professional owners at the end of the eighteenth century? Their number were clearly growing, whilst the widening opportunities for coastal populations to invest in canal, harbour and dock shares may have detracted some passive investors away from shipping. Although they were still likely to be in a minority, the significance of professional owners to the industry may have been far greater if, as seems likely, many were the sole owners of large fleets. Initial evidence reveals such a group of owners in London.[14] Taking a random run of 300 vessels from the London foreign trade registers for 1787, as many as a quarter had only one owner and two-thirds four or less.[15] Ownership was even more concentrated in Liverpool where half the vessels were owned by only one or two people.[16] The pattern of ownership was becoming less widespread, more capital was now required and, along with it, a greater degree of specialisation.[17] Ownership was more dissipated in Whitehaven where 58% of vessels were owned by thirteen or more people.[18] Thus, the shipowner may have emerged only, or more quickly, in the larger trading centres where there existed a substantial body of enterprising merchants prepared to move into shipping if the market promised good rewards.[19] Moreover, these were also the centres of marine insurance and the commercial coffee houses.[20]

Many coasters were under sole ownership. This was a long term feature of the industry unconnected with the rise of the specialist. Coasters were often of very low value, due to their great age and smallness and therefore were more likely to be within the price range of a single owner. Moreover, since many such vessels tramped around the coast, one would expect the master to be the owner.

What appeared to be happening in the half century after about 1780 was the entrance of a new type of person into the shipping industry, prepared and able to take advantage of the vastly increasing trade of this period. The old fashioned merchant organisation of shipowning was unable to cope with the huge increase in the shipping industry required by the trade expansion and the wartime boom of the period. Shipowning as an independent occupation thus appears as a necessary organisational advance in order to increase the provision of shipping space.

Michael Henley and Son

It is against the background of an emerging shipowning profession in the late eighteenth century that the story of Michael Henley and Son is to be set. There is a great deal of vagueness in our knowledge of shipowning, many things we do not know, much we would like to know. The history of Henley and Son provides many of the answers, at least insofar as one principal firm is concerned.

Michael Henley and his son, Joseph, were London shipowners at Wapping between 1775 and 1830. Michael was born in Derby around 1742 and began his working life by serving an apprenticeship as a Thames waterman and lighterman. By the 1760s he was a London waterman and, soon after, a coal merchant beside the Thames. Over the following decade he made a success of merchanting and in 1775 bought a couple of colliers in which to transport coal from Newcastle to London. In subsequent years he purchased further vessels so that by 1790 he owned nine and by 1805, fifteen. By now his vessels were not only to be found in the coastal coal trade, but also in the Baltic, the Mediterranean and the Atlantic. The firm reached its maximum size with twenty-two vessels in 1810 before declining to only seven by 1815 and just two in 1825. The *Freedom*, lost around 1830, was probably their last vessel. Overall, Henley's owned between 129 and 135 vessels of which maybe thirty were sold within a year for breaking up or speculative gain.

Michael's son, Joseph (1766–1832), became interested in his father's business at a comparatively early age and by the early 1780s was playing an active role in it. Joseph was a shrewd and perceptive businessman, playing a prominent part in the successful expansion of the firm in the first decade of the nineteenth century. By 1806 Michael had retired to Derby and had very little further to do with the business, besides occasional advice to his son. Within a few years Michael grew ill and finally died in September 1813.

Joseph's only son, Joseph Warner, was born in 1793 but showed little interest in the business besides two years spent in his father's office after graduating from Oxford in 1815. Joseph was therefore left to run the business, though with increasing help from a ship broker, Edward Rule, and several clerks. Lack of entrepreneurial continuity within the family, along with a prolonged shipping depression in the mid 1820s, persuaded the ageing Joseph to contract his shipping operations and invest elsewhere.

Joseph had kept the firm's accounts and correspondence in an efficient and carefully organised manner for over fifty years and so it was not surprising that when he retired from Wapping to Waterperry almost the entire papers went with him. These were systematically filed in 116 wooden boxes in the loft of Waterperry House where they laid untouched for nearly 150 years. The collection is huge, containing the voluminous internal correspondence, chiefly incoming, between Henley's and their masters, and external correspondence with business contacts and government departments, principally the Transport Board, the Admiralty and the Navy Board. Many detailed ship's accounts survive, especially disbursements recorded by the master and also account books kept by Henley's, freight and brokerage accounts, charterparties, insurance certificates, manifests and bills of lading. There are also detailed accounts and correspondence with their agents, especially James Kirton of Shields. These include evidence relating to the repair of the firm's vessels. Documentation for the coal trade survives for the early years but most of the shipping correspondence and accounts do not exist before about 1785.

The wealth of material in the Henley archive contrasts to the dearth of information regarding shipping businesses in general before about 1830.[21] Most information is of national, macroeconomic statistics such as parliamentary returns and shipping dues. The Henley collection illuminates practically every aspect of shipowning, offering a literary, qualitative, microeconomic view of the industry. For example, it clearly indicates the means of capital accumulation and the manner in which individual vessels were deployed, something which is hardly available in any other source. Even our macroeconomic statistics are intermittent and the Henley evidence can supplement them in relation to such variables as wages and freight rates.

The Henley papers, then, provide a unique day to day view of the operations of an early shipowner, indicating the nature of his approach to his business and the type of policies he pursued. In addition, the Henley experience serves to overcome several grey areas of maritime history. A decade ago, Ralph Davis analysed the progress of maritime historiography and concluded that, 'there is no synthesis dealing with the later eighteenth and nineteenth centuries'[22] and that further research was required in 'the organisation of shipowning and the operation of ships over the previous century, about 1760–1860, which has been so little explored'[23] as well as the 'much neglected history of short-sea and coastal shipping'.[24] Given Henley's close involvement in the coal trade in these years, many gaps can now be filled.

There is a fundamental problem in writing the history of a single firm: how typical was it? A rudimentary analysis of the shipping registers indicates a great diversity in the nature of ownership: there was no typical shipowner. We do know, however, that Henley's were a notable example of a growing group of specialist owners within the industry, shipowners who could be identified by their sole ownership of vessels and the full-time professional attitude they adopted towards shipowning. In the absence of other business records we have no real method of knowing how typical Henley's were even within this group but at least they survived. Indeed, it may well be that the specialist shipowners, professional and informed in their approach, benefited more than the general merchants from the opportunities offered by the war economy. Was it the specialists who survived and the general merchants who fell by the wayside?

How important were Henley's within the shipping industry? At their peak they owned at least twenty vessels, comprising nearly 6,000 tons, which represented 1% of London registered shipping. Given the wide range of ownership, there could only be a limited number of firms as large or larger than Henley's. At Liverpool, some men were involved in the ownership of as much tonnage as Henley's but held only part shares in vessels, the proportion of which was unknown before 1824. Henley's shared ownership of just twelve vessels and none was retained above six years. Ten were shared with only the master and one also with a variety of merchants from England and the West Indies. The *Duke of Clarence*, the only vessel in which Henley's were simply passive investors, was owned jointly with a series of London tradesmen. Although they were sole owners, much of their fleet was old and therefore of low value.

A cursory glance at the London registers suggests that the name Henley appeared as frequently as any other.[25] In fact other owners can be identified who were similar to Henley's in owning vessels outright though between 1786 and 1789 none registered more vessels or tonnage than Henley's. During these years Henley's registered fourteen vessels with an aggregate tonnage of 3,288. Their nearest competitor was James Mather who registered twelve vessels (3,264 tons) of which he was sole owner of eleven. James Margetson registered nine vessels (2,212 tons) as sole owner. Both were London merchants, as were most of the principal sole owners. These men shared other characteristics with Henley's. Both had comparatively old fleets, therefore having a low capital value per ship. Of vessels whose age was known, only one of Mather's ten and one of Margetson's four were less than ten years old and the average age of their fleets was twenty and fourteen years respectively. Also like Henley they took full advantage of the availability of prizes or cheap American vessels, seven of Mather's vessels and six of Margetson's fell into these categories. On the other hand, neither owner had a single vessel built in the North-East, in contrast to Henley's, which suggests they had little or no interest in the coal trade. Two-thirds of Mather's vessels were between 200 and 400 tons. This was the size of vessel favoured by Henley's because it was regarded as suitable for deployment in many trades. The size of Margetson's vessels was more varied; two-thirds of his vessels were prizes which suggested that he laid more stress upon cheapness rather than construction to a particular design or size.

Sixteen of the twenty-six major sole owners at London, 1786–9, called themselves simply merchants. Each of the remaining ten had a different occupation, namely timber merchant, corn factor, coal factor, malster, ship broker, coal undertaker, mariner, boat builder, shipwright and coal merchant (Henley). Looking at the lesser sole owners who only possessed a vessel or two, merchants again predominate although there are more mariners and a further four coal merchants. All this suggests Henley's were far from atypical and certainly some of the 'merchants' would have dealt in coal.

Where Henley's may have been different from many London owners was in their degree of concentration upon the coastal coal trade. Six or seven times as much London owned shipping was to be found in the port's foreign trade as in its coasting, in spite of the greater aggregate size of London's coastal trade.[26] This is mainly explained by the large number of northern mine owners, fitters and agents who invested in colliers trading to London. Henley's, with their concentration on the coal trade for many years, appear to have acted more like outport owners. In the early years of the nineteenth century they increasingly diversified into the foreign trades, which may have made them more typical of London owners.

Evidence from Henley's bills of sale confirms the existence of similar sole owners in London. In July 1801, Henley's bought the *Neptune* from Patrick Simpson, who called himself a Southwark shipowner[27] and in May 1810 *Oeconomy* was bought from William Havelock, a Greenhithe shipowner.[28] Often vessels were bought from 'merchants' who may have been specialist shipowners. Former Henley masters, James Kirton and William Dodds, began to act as shipowners during the French Wars.

Literary references within the Henley papers imply that the firm was important and held influence within London's maritime community and in government circles. Moreover, Joseph was a member of Lloyds and the family came to own an impressive country house near Oxford along with their substantial premises in Wapping and several other parts of London. Therefore, the firm must be regarded as one of the larger and more successful shipowners in London.

Henley's were also large in comparison with many firms in other industries. The textile industry has for long been regarded as central to Britain's early phase of industrialisation.[29] Henley's employed more capital than was used in most cotton mills and this will be discussed further in the next chapter. The average Manchester cotton mill employed less than 130 people in 1803, a figure surpassed by Henley's for much of their existence.[30]

The shipping industry in war and peace

Besides its unique contribution to the issue of the professional shipowner, the Henley experience throws a torchlight upon macroeconomic developments within the shipping industry in a period about which historians know little. This was an important period for three reasons. To begin with it composed the final half century before the emergence of steam shipping. Since steam took so long to diffuse through the industry one must ask whether this is explained by the increased efficiency and competitiveness of sail. Secondly, this was a period of intermittent warfare; quite clearly the wars had a substantial influence upon the development of the industry. Thirdly, this was the first and critical phase of Britain's industrialisation and one would wish to investigate the significance of the shipping industry to this process.

Shipping was important to the economy through its linkages with many other industries, especially shipbuilding, iron, copper, coal, timber, armaments and many traded commodities. In an island nation, shipping was essential for trade and communications; it facilitated international specialisation and enabled exploration and settlement. The capital of shipping was large and 'lumped' and, therefore, changes in the demand for shipping would reverberate through the economy by the 'accelerator' effect. The nature of investment in shipping offered some limitation on liability through Admiralty law and enabled relatively small investors to take part. The high profits generated in the industry during the wars at the end of the eighteenth century could be ploughed back into the economy through the 'multiplier' effect. Shipping was a large employer of labour.[31] Finally, shipping was an example of an early service industry and made an important and enduring contribution to the invisibles account of the balance of payments.[32]

The size of the mercantile marine doubled between 1786 and the end of the French Wars to reach a peak of 2·6 million tons which was not surpassed for another twenty-five years.[33] From a qualitative perspective, the period witnessed the development of the agency system,[34] improvements in business accounting and the growing importance of the north-east ports as centres of shipbuilding and the coal trade. These together with the increased productivity of shipping, changes in its deployment, rising freight rates, profits and wages and the growth of marine insurance were all significant developments illustrated in the Henley papers. In a wider context, the progress made by the shipping industry was part of the general improvements in the transport infrastructure of the economy. The acceleration of the construction of canals, river navigations, roads and docks were all part of this development offering the industrialising economy cheaper, quicker, more regular transport which would serve to integrate the market and make industry more footloose.[35]

During the wars of the late eighteenth century, the demand for shipping rose, largely as a consequence of the expansion of the transport service which used as much as ten per cent of the mercantile marine in its operations. Simultaneously, supply was constricted by the delaying effects of the convoy system and the timber shortage, exacerbated by the blockade of the Baltic. Even at the best of times, inelastic supply conditions in the shipbuilding industry meant that the volume of shipping could only be expanded by 2 or 3% per annum in response to rising demand. This scissors movement of supply and demand had implications for many aspects of shipping. It exerted considerable pressure upon the supply of seamen, port facilities and the construction and repair of vessels causing bottlenecks and rising costs. On the other hand, freight rates increased and allowed enterprising shipowners to earn large profits. War was particularly important for easing or provoking the emergence of the specialist shipowner, as was noted above. Vicissitudes in the level of military activity meant rapid and volatile movements in such shipping indices as wages, profits, freight rates and ship prices upon which the shipowner had to make prompt though considered judgements. Frequently, it was the ability to make these responses which distinguished success from failure amongst shipowners.

The transport service guaranteed regular employment and earnings on a time charter normally for at least three months and compensation was paid if the vessel was captured. On the other hand, payments were often delayed and the subsequent cash flow problems inhibited the exploitation of more lucrative alternative trading opportunities. Delays in releasing vessels could have a similar effect. Transports were often left waiting around in Mediterranean ports for many months, rendering them vulnerable to bad weather and 'worming' and resulting in large repair bills. Masters of transports had to adhere to strict and comparatively high manning ratios or face deductions from freight earnings.

Convoys, by slowing down vessel movements, served to constrict the supply of shipping thus reinforcing the bottlenecks and increasing the costs and earnings which were mentioned in relation to rising demand. The size and efficiency of the convoy system grew during the eighteenth century[36] and by the time of the French Wars convoys were available in the coastal as well as foreign trades, though coasting masters were often reluctant to wait around for convoys over such short distances. However, the dangers of coasting were great and caused Henley's frequently to remind their masters that coastal convoys would be provided if vessels stopped at Yarmouth on their passage south. A Convoy Act of 1798[37] stipulated that all vessels in the foreign trades had to sail in convoy unless they were East Indiamen, Hudson Bay Company vessels, on passages to Ireland or vessels deemed to be sufficiently fast and protected to sail independently as a 'runner'. Henleys had licences for several vessels to sail separately including the *Aurora* which possessed ten carriage guns and a crew of twelve. Convoys still had a tendency to break up in bad weather which was the cause of the capture of several Henley vessels. In 1805 *Hermes* became separated from a convoy in a storm and sailed to Madeira, the rendezvous point. None of the fleet was there so the master sailed on alone only to be captured near Martinique.

The development of the convoy system went hand in hand with that of marine insurance and it is not surprising to find Lloyds supporting the Admiralty in enforcing convoy discipline.[38] Both these factors encouraged the specialist by mitigating some of the risks of wartime which otherwise threatened to negate the benefits of high profits. By slowing down ship movements at sea, convoys favoured the use of flat bottomed vessels which were slow but capacious. By bunching vessels together both at the port of departure and arrival, convoys put great pressure upon all port facilities from dock and wharf space to the availability of provisions and labour. As such this may have contributed to the construction of many new docks at London during the French Wars.[39]

References

1. For example, see R. Jarvis, 'Eighteenth century London shipping' in A. Hollaender & W. Kellaway (eds.), *Studies in London History*, London, 1969, pp. 414–17.
2. This restricted the formation of joint stock companies following the South Sea Company fiasco.
3. G. Jackson, *Hull in the Eighteenth Century*, London, 1972, p. 140. Moreover, ownership of a few shares in different ships would enable a merchant more effectively to secure shipping space when he required it.

4. See R. Jarvis, 'Ship registry – 1786', *Maritime History*, IV, 1974, pp. 12–28.

5. Anon, *The Late Measures of the Shipowners in the Coal Trade*, London, 1786, p. 15.

6. R. Davis, *The Rise of the English Shipping Industry in the Seventeenth and Eighteenth Centuries*, London, 1962, p. 81. Though the term shipowner was used in the Newcastle shipping registers from 1786 onwards, Tyne and Wear Record Office, 1253.

7. *Ibid.*, pp. 88–9.

8. Lloyd's developed rapidly in the eighteenth century partly under the influence of war which acted both as a stimulus to underwriting and necessitated improvements in methods in order to survive uncertain times. Lloyd's agency system developed and underwriters' associations were formed in ports such as Bristol, Hull, Liverpool and Newcastle. C. Wright & C. Fayle, *A History of Lloyd's*, London, 1928, chs. 7–14. Mutual insurance clubs of shipowners grew up at London and in the north-east.

9. Anon, *Late Measures*, p. 4.

10. *Ibid.*, pp. 5–6.

11. G. Jackson, *British Whaling Trade*, London, 1978, pp. 70–1. The ending of the American war prevented direct American competition and encouraged firms like the Enderbys from Boston to settle in Britain as shipowners.

12. Jackson, *Hull*, pp. 142–3.

13. R. Davis, 'Maritime history: progress and problems', in S. Marriner (ed.), *Business and Businessmen*, Liverpool, 1978, pp. 171–3.

14. Although it does not necessarily follow that the sole ownership of a vessel was accompanied by its management or a concentration of business interests into shipping by its owner, it is highly likely, especially if the entrepreneur owned a series of vessels.

15. Jarvis, 'London shipping', p. 414.

16. R. Craig & R. Jarvis, *Liverpool Registry of Merchant Ships*, Manchester, 1967, tables 24 and 25.

17. Anon, *Late Measures*, pp. 15–16.

18. Jarvis, 'London shipping', p. 417.

19. Significantly, merchants comprised a half of shipping investors in London and 80% in Liverpool, though only 15% in Whitehaven. *Ibid.*, p. 417.

20. The reverse argument is that in the smaller ports, with fewer opportunities for merchanting, more entrepreneurs were solely shipowners. However, there were alternative opportunities especially in ancillary trades like sailmaking and ship chandling. But were there sufficient merchanting opportunities from which an individual could expand his capital investments into shipowning? Obviously

many people in the outports bought shares in ships but it is less certain that many of them became professional shipowners at this time.

21. For example, F. E. Hyde, *Blue Funnel: A History of Alfred Holt and Company of Liverpool, 1865–1914*, Liverpool, 1957; G. Blake, *The Ben Line, 1825–1955*, London, 1956; R. S. McLellan, *Anchor Line, 1856–1956*, Glasgow, 1956; L. Cope Cornford, *A Century of Sea Trading, 1824–1924. The General Steam Navigation Company Limited*, London, 1924. All these begin at the end of or after the Henley period.

22. Davis, 'Maritime History', pp. 169–70.

23. *Ibid.*, pp. 176–7.

24. *Ibid.*, p. 177.

25. Public Record Office (P.R.O.), Board of Trade/107.

26. P.R.O., Customs 36/5.

27. HNL/25/81. How people chose to describe themselves might be a matter of custom and usage rather than a careful distinction of function.

28. HNL/25/92.

29. For example, see S. D. Chapman, *The Early Cotton Masters*, Newton Abbot, 1967, pp. 126, 128; C. H. Lee, *A Cotton Enterprise, 1795–1840*, Manchester, 1972, p. 102.

30. R. S. Fitton & A. R. Wadsworth, *The Strutts and the Arkwrights, 1758–1830*, Manchester, 1958, p. 192.

31. Davis, 'Maritime History', p. 179 suggests that seamen constituted 3 or 4% of the adult male population around 1750.

32. See A. Imlah, *Economic Elements in the Pax Britannica*, Cambridge, Mass., 1958.

33. G. Chalmers, *The State of the United Kingdom at the Peace of Paris, November 20, 1815*, London, 1816, p. 12. Some of the increase is illusory due to the failure of the registrars of shipping at individual ports always to eliminate tonnage wrecked, captured, missing or broken up.

34. See R. B. Westerfield, *Middlemen in English Business*, New Haven, Conn., 1915 and S. Ville, 'James Kirton, shipping agent', *Mariner's Mirror*, LXVII, 1981, pp. 149–62.

35. See the various chapters in D. H. Aldcroft & M. Freeman (eds.), *Transport in the Industrial Revolution*, Manchester, 1983.

36. P. Crowhurst, *The Defence of British Trade, 1689–1815*, Folkestone, 1977, p. 80. Convoys could sometimes be as large as 600 merchant vessels and more than thirty escorting naval ships.

37. 38 Geo. III, c. 76.

38. HNL/72/12.

39. See W. M. Stern, 'The first London dock boom and the growth of the West India docks', *Economica*, new ser., XIX, 1952, pp. 59–77.

2 · Capital accumulation and business formation

Michael Henley began his working life as a Thames waterman. By the 1760s he was merchanting coal, first at Shadwell and later at Wapping. By the following decade the business was growing rapidly; in 1773 he handled around 2,100 chaldrons of coal and 3,700[1] two years later. Profits were ploughed back in order to expand the capital of the business, for example barges and lighters were purchased to facilitate the transfer of coal from onboard colliers for sale to customers or to Henley's own stocks. Several buildings were purchased so too were materials or goodwill from other businesses. In 1775 two collier vessels, the *Henley* and the *Mary*, were purchased. Together they could deliver about 2,700 chaldrons in a year, thus adding considerably to the capacity of the business. Although old and relatively small, the vessels required a large capital outlay for a coal merchant and initiated an important change of direction of the business, enabling Henley's to import their own coal from Newcastle rather than purchase it in the Pool of London. Vertical integration of shipowning and merchanting was a common feature of the coal trade. Since the voyage was short and coal relatively uniform and durable, the specialised knowledge required to carry and merchant it was minimal and regular, accurate information easy to obtain. It was also the result of the high ratio of transport costs to total costs. Thus integration was a comparatively simple development and means of expansion promising potentially higher profits, by taking both the shipowner and merchant's share. It also enabled greater control of the market in a trade dogged by competing groups of colliery owners, shipowners and merchants keen to secure their share of profits.

However, coal merchanting continued to dominate their expanding business through the 1780s and by the outbreak of the French Wars, 30,000 chaldrons passed through their hands annually.[2] They were not averse to dabbling in other profitable activities. In 1773 Michael bought the capital and goodwill of John Fowler, a dealer in sand,[3] and was also working as a lighterman and making money from ownership of a wharf. He also dealt in ship's stores; for example, in 1790 he made money from buying and selling anchors.[4] Shipbreaking was yet another activity. In 1788 he bought the *Surprise*, sold her stores individually and part-exchanged the hull for another vessel.[5] The diversity of his business interests are reflected in the variety of occupations attributed to him in the London directories. In 1780 he was described as a merchant, in 1793 as a coal merchant and in 1802 there were two entries, one as 'Henley and Son, coal merchants' and the other as 'Henley Michael and Son, shipowners'.[6] In a tax document of 1783 Michael is referred to as a lighterman, wharfinger and dealer in ropes,[7] whilst a decade later he was described as a coal merchant and dealer in ship's stores.[8]

The watershed in the evolution of the firm occurred in the 1790s when coal merchanting and most ancillary activities were abandoned in favour of a concentration upon shipowning. Within a few years of the beginning of the nineteenth century Henley's no longer merchanted coal though they still employed vessels in the coal trade and sold their cargoes to merchants. Indeed, they viewed the coal trade as a backbone to their shipping business because it offered relatively reliable rates of return, flexibility of deployment, being a short haul, and contact with a port, Newcastle, renowned for the quality of shipbuilding and repair together with the size of its market in second-hand vessels. Their fleet was expanded and vessels were now deployed in a diversity of trades. Many of the explanations of the rise of specialist shipowning which were discussed in the previous chapter are a feature of the Henley experience as will be seen in more detail later. Above all, the prospect of high profits, which was a feature of wartime shipowning, drew Henley's into the industry. By the 1790s Michael had been in business during two major wars and was keenly aware of their impact upon the shipping industry. It is true that wartime profits must be set against large losses and bankruptcies experienced by some shipowners, though a man of his business acumen and experience could be reasonably hopeful of substantial gains. Joseph, who was active in the business from the 1780s, did not have his father's specialised interest in the coal trade and so diversification was likely. This was a suitable means of development from an operation requiring a relatively small capital base to one of larger investments.

When did Henley's first consider themselves specialist ship-owners? It was probably sometime in the 1790s. Among the registrations of their vessels, they are not cited as shipowners until 1816,[9] although in a tax return for 1808 Michael described the business as, 'Michael Henley and Son, Ship Owners and Merchants'.[10] From 1806, when Michael retired to Derby, a regular correspondence developed between him and Joseph, which made it clear that the business was overwhelmingly orientated towards shipowning. This was a response to wartime market conditions, 'we cannot make more of our money than in good shipping,'[11] wrote Michael in November, 1806.

The conversion to shipowning was the only major structural change in the business. After 1815 shipping faced a major and prolonged postwar depression, largely because the supply of vessels outstretched the demand for them. Henley's therefore withdrew their capital from the industry and probably invested it in government stock or industrial portfolios. Lack of entrepreneurial continuity within the family prevented them from altering the nature of their business a second time.

The initial sources of finance for the business are not wholly clear. Few institutional sources of finance for industry existed in the eighteenth century. Michael may have received money by way of an inheritance or through marrying into a rich family, though the evidence is inconclusive. Successful property speculation around Wapping in the 1780s may have yielded further finance for expansion.[12]

Henley's rarely used 'sleeping partners' to raise finance for shipping. A handful of vessels were briefly shared with reputable masters who were given greater responsibility in that vessel's operation. Sole ownership may have been a function of the professional shipowner who wished to be thoroughly independent, accountable to no-one and able to take all the decisions as and when he wished. However, throughout both the eighteenth and nineteenth centuries there existed entrepreneurs who managed vessels, either as single ship operations or as an overall enterprise, where ownership was largely vested in sleeping partners. What appears to be significant about Henley's experience is that they saw no need to raise further capital from outside. Their early business activities required little capital and this was gradually developed by ploughing back profits. By the time they began to convert to shipowning, they possessed sufficient resources to finance the purchase of old, cheap vessels. Rather than a capital shortage, their problem was to find sufficient suitable vessels to exploit the wartime boom fully. To have taken on sleeping partners would have left them with a range of undesirable options either to reduce their own investments in a profitable

period or to struggle with an unwieldly enterprise of thirty or
more vessels or to delegate managerial responsibility. The resort
to sleeping partners was more suited to the owner with little
finance of his own or who was more interested in purchasing new
vessels for the valuable commodity trades. Nor did Henley's
mortgage vessels to raise finance.

The size of the capital stock and its rate of formation were
considerable in the shipping industry and help to explain its
important role in the industrialisation of Britain. Shipping was
a heavily capitalised industry at the end of the eighteenth century
and, indeed, was one of the country's chief users of capital;
around £100 of capital was employed for every seaman on
board.[13] However, the size and rate of capital formation in
shipping have been underrated by historians[14] because of their
neglect of the social overhead capital of the industry, such as
quays and wharves. Nor has allowance been made for the amount
of capital used by firms aside from that embodied in the vessels.
This point is all the more significant given the emergence of the
professional shipowner who may have used more shipping
related capital in his business than the 'general merchant'.
Indeed, one of the most valuable aspects of the Henley experience
is the unique evidence which survives concerning their shore-
based assets and liquid capital.

The most important form of fixed capital was the vessels
themselves. Table six shows the aggregate tonnage of the Henley
fleet from the mid 1780s when the 1786 Registration Act and the
more comprehensive information in the firm's archive makes it
possible to give accurate results.[15] Before 1790, Henley's owned,
on average, half a dozen vessels simultaneously, and most were
sold after only a few years ownership. The firm was active in the
ship market in 1784 and 1785, buying six vessels in the first year
and seven in the second. Many were soon resold, suggesting
speculation on a rising market after the postwar depression. Ten
vessels were brought in 1788 in the expectation of prosperous
wartime trading. Joseph had noted the previous October, 'at
present all is for warr in London',[16] but he was proved wrong
and had to resell. By 1791 Britain was unquestionably on the eve
of war and so the firm bought five more vessels, including
two new ones. The long term use of these vessels suggests
Henley's no longer regarded shipowning as a speculative adjunct

of merchanting. Further acquisitions in 1793–4 were financed by rising profits at the beginning of the war. The misfortune of losing five vessels to the enemy between 1795 and 1797 restricted further growth before the end of the decade. Three had been transports and therefore compensation was paid though only much later.

The return to war in 1803 encouraged a further expansion of their shipping; eight vessels were bought in that year, five in the following and four in 1805. Some were kept only a short while and were intended for breaking up or speculative resale. However, many were bought with long-term use in mind or for specific employment following, for example, the agreement of a transport service contract. Expansion was slower in the next few years as Henley's concentrated their time on breaking into the Atlantic trades, where more capital was required to fit out vessels. A further flurry of activity on the ship market occurred in 1810–12, during which time the firm bought nineteen vessels and sold fourteen. Of a total of twelve shared ownership ships, six were bought between 1809 and 1811 and were shared with long standing masters as a means of delegating some managerial responsibility, raising extra capital and spreading risks. Aggregate tonnage reached its peak of 5,934 in 1810 but this had collapsed to only 2,536 tons by 1815 as Henley's wisely sold out in advance of the postwar depression. Speculating on the hope of a rising market, they bought five vessels cheaply in 1816 but conditions remained depressed and they waited until a temporary boom in 1824–5 before selling up most of the remainder of their fleet.

Table six contains an estimate of the capital value of the Henley fleet over time in constant prices. Accepting Feinstein's figure of £20 per ton for the price of new shipping, 1801–20,[17] suitable deductions for depreciation have been made according to the age of the Henley fleet.[18] The index indicates a sudden, large expansion in the value of the fleet in the 1780s as Henley's began to buy up vessels for speculative reasons. The expansion of the fleet during wartime is offset by its increasing age and therefore its overall value barely rises until 1809–10 when there is a marked growth in the number of vessels. After 1817 the size of the fleet contracts and the average age increases, leading to a sustained decline in its aggregate capital value.

They also owned fixed capital in the form of spare stores for vessels. Henley's kept spare deck stores in a 'store house' and extra sails in a sail loft. The precise extent of these is unknown though they were probably of some considerable size, especially when the firm was at its most active. When a vessel was being fitted out for a long voyage, the store and loft were drawn upon heavily, sometimes £500 or more of stores were withdrawn. All types of ship's equipment were kept in the store, including salted provisions. As the size of their fleet expanded, Henley's built up these reserves. There were notable advantages to buying reserves of stores rather than paying the spot price, which might be higher, as the materials were required. Henley's bought second-hand stores at bargain prices in public sales and auctions organised to dispose of the assets of bankrupts or the remainders of wrecks. From Henley's notes on auction sheets, it is clear that a small group of shipowners purchased most of these stores, suggesting that they were pursuing similar policies.

Considering the rate at which Henley's bought stores gives some idea of the size of their warehouses.[19] (Table 1.) The French Wars enabled Henley's to build up their stock of ship's materials by buying stores belonging to prizes or badly damaged vessels. The accounts dealing with the store house are very sporadic and only cover the period 1782 to 1795 in any detail.[20] Account books relating to the sail loft survive only for 1789–90 and 1813–20.[21] We know that as early as November 1775 Michael was buying stores at auctions at Sheerness.[22]

In building up their stores, Henley's took advantage of cheap labour at the local workhouses,[23] paying 3s per hundredweight to have old rope and junk picked into oakum and the same for oakum to be knotted into yarn by the workhouses of Wapping, Aldgate, St George's and St Sepulchre's.[24] Wapping Workhouse alone provided them with 289 hundredweight of oakum and yarn between July 1786 and July 1781.[25] Unfortunately, surviving account books only give weights and not values.[26] (Table 2.)

Annual stocktaking accounts for the sail loft between 1815 and 1819 give some idea of the size of their stocks. In May 1815, Henley's valued their sail loft at £1,010[27] ánd in July 1817, at £476.[28] A year later this had fallen to £307[29] but increased twelve months later to £464.[30] With the business contracting at this time, the value of sails in the loft was probably much higher in about 1810 or 1812. The very large size of their loft is suggested

Table 1. *Purchases of ship's equipment, 1780–1822*

Year	Amount (£)
1780	184
1781	383
1782	171
1783	287
1784	738
1785	410
1787	314
1788	610
1790	710
1791	188
1792	62
1793	64
1794	33
1796	847
1797	389
1798	582
1799	452
1800	— various priced items
1802	191
1803	179
1804	212
1805	13
1819	22
1822	204

Table 2. *Weight of rope, oakum and yarn owned, 1782–90*

Year	Weight (cwt)
1782	730
1783	560
1784	162
1785	584
1786	425
1787	292
1788	56
1789	141
1790	111

by what evidence does survive. For example, Robert Hunter, a sailmaker of Whitby, supplied Henley's with nearly £900 worth of goods between November 1803 and February 1807.[31] Further intimations of size are given by some informal notes written by Joseph Henley.[32] (Table 3.) Conceivably, these figures may

Table 3. *Valuation of warehouse and sail loft, 1805–14*

Year		£	s	d	
1805–6		740	4	2	Warehouse
		330	10	11	Sail loft
		1,070	15	1	
1807–8		1,806	3	2	Sail loft & warehouse
1809		1,394	3	4	Sail loft & warehouse
1810		269	11	6	Sail loft & warehouse
1811	Dr	3,382	3	8	
1812	Cr	2,969	3	1	
1813	Cr	1,010	0	10	
1814	Cr	665	2	6	

indicate the value of the stocks in the sail and loft warehouse although the figures for 1810 and 1813 are lower than that for the stock of just the sail loft in 1815 when the firm's operations were much smaller. In addition, the warehouse of other ship's stores could be expected to be of at least twice the value of the sail loft, as suggested by the figure for 1805–6 above. The use of 'Dr' and 'Cr' against some of these figures suggest that they were balances, probably the difference between the amount of stores received into the warehouse through purchases and the value of stores leaving their stock to be used on board their vessels. On an adjoining piece of paper[33] two more figures are given, £4,582 14s 0d and £7,933 16s 7d with no explanation. Possibly, they were the value of the stock in two different years or, alternatively, the smaller sum was the sail loft and the larger the warehouse at a particular date. Either way the combined value of the sail loft and the warehouse of stores at the height of the business, around 1810–12, was unlikely to have been less than about £6,000.

Henley's also held capital in the form of river craft to support the loading and unloading of their vessels, especially in the coal trade. These boats were also used in the merchanting side of the business, especially in the early years. Once again the precise number and value which they owned is not known from year to year. However, by 1781[34] and 1783[35] they owned at least five and possessed fifteen in 1800. This made Henley's one of the largest boat owners on the Thames. Below London Bridge there were 81 owners of a total of 429 craft, with Henley's being the fourth largest owner,[36] confirming their important role in the coal trade. They are known to have bought the craft shown in Table 4.[37] Again, some items are missing. Given the figure of fifteen craft owned in 1800, they probably owned about £800 to £1,000 worth of capital in this form.

Table 4.   *Purchases of river craft, 1772–1807*

Year	Purchases	Cost		
		£	s	d
1772	1 barge	100	0	0
1774	2 barges	127	15	6
1775	2 lighters	29	0	0
1778	2 punts	63	0	0
1780	4 coal craft			
	2 lighters			
	2 punts	249	14	0
1785	1 barge	35	0	0
1786	1 barge	63	0	0
1793	4 barges	279	10	0
1794	2 coal craft	46	0	0
1807	1 punt	65	0	0

A related form of capital was stocks of coal. Thomas Hawkes[38] claimed that he had room on his wharf to store 2,000–3,000 chaldrons of coal; conceivably, Henley's could have done the same, though they would probably have disposed of their coal as soon as possible rather than tie up money in this form.

Henley's owned a good deal of property in Wapping including three houses, numbers 341 – 3 Wapping, three or four warehouses, the Crooked Billet Inn, a bakehouse, a 'counting house', one or two wharves and possibly several other properties. The problem is to value the properties and decide which should be included in a capital assessment of the business. The three houses can probably be discounted but was the Crooked Billet of some value to the business? There is no extant evidence that they acted as undertakers to hire dock labour in the coal trade or were involved in crimping. Sometimes they hired undertakers and crimps themselves. Perhaps they rented the property to such people. The wharves should probably be included though these were sometimes rented out to other merchants. For example, John Turnbridge, a coal and corn merchant, rented 'Henley's wharf' between 1800 and 1803 at the cost of a guinea a week,[39] though he may not have had exclusive rights over its use.

An evaluation of the properties is more difficult to achieve. Michael Henley bought various properties from John Fowler, a sand dealer, in 1773, though these only amounted to £220 in value.[40] Many of Henley's properties were built between 1779 and 1786. Although a number of accounts survive, it is difficult to distinguish between building costs and subsequent repairs. In 1779 bills amounting to £2,520 were paid in connection with building work of all forms on three houses, various walls and several wharves owned by Henley's.[41] In the next seven or eight years there were bills for work on these properties amounting to at least £5,000.[42] An insurance policy of January 1794 cites three warehouses insured for a total sum of £2,000, a house and warehouse at 343 Wapping at £800, another house at £400 and another warehouse at £400.[43] However, one does not know how accurate the valuations were and whether Henley's insured for the full value. The second part of this problem is possibly solved by Henley's insurance notes for 1796, which were set out as shown in Table 5.[44] The figure on the left is probably the value of the properties and the one on the right that proportion for which they were insured. In which case it is interesting to reflect that the full value of the warehouses alone was insured. It seems that Henley's also owned a warehouse attached to 343 Wapping.[45]

Table 5. *Valuation of premises, 1796*

Amount (£)	Property	Amount (£)
2,000	Premises 341, 342	900
1,000	Goods therein	700
2,500	Premises, 343	1,600
1,200	Goods therein	1,100
1,000	Crooked billet and bake house	800
2,400	Warehouses	2,400
10,100		7,500

In addition, a letter written in June 1811 suggested that they owned a 'large stack of warehouses opposite Briant's wharf at the Hermitage'.[46] Unfortunately, there is no valuation for the wharves, though they were probably not worth more than £1,000. The value of the counting house is unknown, whilst it is unclear whether the Crooked Billet Inn was an integral part of the business or not. Probably the total value of the business-related capital in property was around £5,000 in 1800.

Consequently, at the end of the eighteenth century Henley's owned about £6,000 of capital in buildings and river craft. A figure for capital in spare stores is not known until at least half a decade later. Taking account of inflation and the large expansion of the firm between these years, this capital in 1800 must have been worth around £3,000. A new vessel built in the north-east cost about £13 per ton in 1800. Therefore, if one deducts a third from the figure in Table 6 based upon £20 per ton at constant prices, it gives an approximate value of the Henley fleet, in current prices, as £18,000 in 1800. Thus one can see a ratio of fixed capital in vessels, to that in buildings, spare stores and craft of 2:1.

Some important points emerge from these findings. They add to our understanding of the capital structure of businesses, especially the growth of their fixed and overhead capital, in the age of industrialisation.[47] Secondly, current estimates of the capital embodied in the shipping industry at the end of the eighteenth century may underestimate by up to a third the true level because of the concealment of much fixed capital, especially in the form of buildings and spare stores. This is most clearly

Table 6.   *Fleet size, aggregate tonnage, average age and computed value, 1783–1830*

Date	Ships	Tonnage	Average age[a]	Computed Value (£ s)
1783	2	428	15	4,923
1784	3	670	13	7,822
1785	6	1813	10	24,555
1786	7	2189	11	28,045
1787	8	2476	12	30,431
1788	14	3403	13	40,053
1789	9	2793	15	30,795
1790	9	2793	16	29,630
1791	11	3153	13	41,420
1792	9	2596	11	35,674
1793	10	2749	8	40,339
1794	11	3035	9	43,304
1795	11	3023	13	38,111
1796	11	3011	11	38,033
1797	8	2150	13	25,394
1798	8	2087	16	21,993
1799	9	2443	14	28,339
1800	9	2548	15	28,099
1801	11	3044	15	32,721
1802	10	2767	15	30,465
1803	13	3629	17	35,407
1804	15	4432	18	42,134
1805	15	4301	19	39,146
1806	14	4186	15	41,976
1807	14	4237	16	40,920
1808	16	4628	15	45,998
1809	19	5232	16	49,512
1810	22	5934	16	56,477
1811	20	5907	19	47,789
1812	19	5677	17	48,578
1813	14	4388	19	35,444
1814	11	3515	18	31,118
1815	7	2536	21	19,574
1816	12	4407	23	33,535
1817	12	4407	24	31,732
1818	11	4184	26	28,092
1819	10	3694	23	26,958
1820	9	3433	26	21,625
1821	9	3416	27	20,417
1822	8	3026	28	16,396
1823	8	3026	29	15,618
1824	3	1087	36	3,629
1825	2	719	32	2,580
1826	2	719	33	2,580
1827	2	719	34	2,190
1828	2	719	35	2,190
1829	2	719	36	2,190
1830	2	719	37	2,190

Note (a) The age of several vessels is unknown. They have been given the average age of the fleet in that particular year. The effect on the results is marginal.

illustrated by reference to professional shipowners like Henley's who were likely to have a high demand for such ancillary capital.

Such conclusions suggest that the shipping industry, in relation to capital formation at least, played a more central role in the industrialisation of Britain than has been hitherto assumed. Henley's capital requirements far exceeded a textile firm like Oldknowe, Cowpe & Co. who employed only £10,000 of fixed capital in 1799.[48] However, much depends upon how efficiently this capital was employed; possibly the shipping industry may have diverted scarce investment away from other, more productive, areas of the economy and therefore retarded the process of industrialisation. Measuring capital productivity in the shipping industry is very difficult. The use of convoys during intermittent warfare in the eighteenth and early nineteenth centuries slowed down vessel movements and so may have reduced the efficiency of the industry. On the other hand, several historians have drawn attention to the secular growth of productivity in the industry in the seventeenth and eighteenth centuries.[49] Moreover, the long life span of Henley's vessels, along with the high rates of return on capital, suggests its comparatively efficient use.

Working capital is the most elusive, in definition, and least investigated form of capital. It consists of items used up in the process of production such as raw materials and labour. Even Feinstein's detailed examination of capital in the period of industrialisation, barely touches the issue.[50] For shipowners working capital included wages, victuals, small running repairs, light and harbour dues, the purchase of coal and other miscellaneous items consumed in the course of a voyage.

With working capital an effective interest charge is incurred for the time elapsing between the purchase of these goods and the receipt of the revenue from the enterprise. With the exception of advance and monthly money, wages were paid at the end of the voyage and, therefore, shortly before the receipt of freight revenue. On the other hand, salted provisions and other fitting out items were put on board at the beginning of the voyage. Credit was generally given on the revenue and cost sides but a large operator like Henley's, with a great deal of business to conduct, probably commanded sufficient loyalty from small tradesmen, reliant upon their patronage, to be a net beneficiary from this system. More working capital was required in the coal trade since

Henley's also bought and sold the cargo. Frequently, the promise of regular patronage of a particular fitter,[51] secured Henley's good credit terms for the cargo. Moreover, the time which elapsed between payment for the cargo, when the vessel was fully loaded at Shields, and its sale, in the Pool of London, was often only a matter of days.

The Industrial Revolution witnessed a large growth in the amount of fixed capital in the economy, though it is dangerous to exaggerate its proportion of total investment. Some of the metallurgical industries had less than a third in fixed capital, whilst the cotton industry was exceptional in rising to just over half its capital in fixed stock.[52] By comparison, Henley's in 1800 owned £27,000 of fixed capital but only £23,000 of working capital, giving a high ratio of 54%. Even allowing for errors or the possible argument that spare stores should be classified as working capital, it is still fixed capital which is the major component of their investments. This ratio is the same as for the cotton industry in this period. In 1800 many Henley vessels were deployed in the coal trade where the amount of working capital employed was much greater than in other trades. As their vessels moved out of the coal trade after 1800, so the proportion of fixed to liquid capital grew further.

In what light did shipowners like Henley's view their capital? They were unlikely to distinguish between these various types of capital. Indeed, they probably only had a vague perception of fixed capital and none at all of working.[53] They did, however, have a strong notion of the value of their vessels, but only as a marketable commodity which they would try and sell at a good price.

Ralph Davis argued that each ship was regarded as a separate enterprise before the evolution of the professional shipowner.[54] It is true that the new specialist shipowner saw the advantages of working his fleet together in order to gain economies of scale, but to what extent did he regard his ships as one overall capital stock? The operation of each vessel was still, in some respects, an isolated enterprise, with individual performances and profits being analysed. This is indicated by the careful accounting and evaluation of stores transferred from one Henley vessel to another.[55] On the other hand, Henley's motive may have been to keep a careful watch on the masters of their ships. Indeed, this may have been the central aim of their accounting policy.

The accounts of the business can be divided into the disbursements kept by masters during each voyage and books of all transactions kept by Henley's in London. In the early years of the business, the accounts were kept in a rather ad hoc and inconsistent manner. However, from about the time of the outbreak of the Napoleonic phase of the wars, the accounts began to take a more rational and consistent shape. This change resulted from Joseph's increasing influence in the firm and the growing size and specialisation of the business, thereby making a logical accounting system imperative. A dual system of 'private ship ledgers' and 'general ledgers' was established. The former consisted of an individual book for each vessel, containing the balance of a master's disbursements for each voyage, cash advanced to him and any items paid for by Henley's in London. The general ledger was normally an annual volume covering all vessels. These are no longer extant so it is unclear whether whole accounts were copied into here or just balances. Freight ledgers were also introduced during the Napoleonic Wars but again the depth of their detail is uncertain since they have not survived. Double entry book-keeping, a central tenet of modern accounting, was developing in this period. Henley's used some aspects of double-entry, especially after 1805. The use of cash and account books for stores and provisions bought by them in London illustrates this, with purchases being noted as a receipt in the account book and a payment in the cash book. The firm seems to have paid little attention to the questionable single entry reforms proposed by Edward Jones in 1795. In the account books which survive they never spread three or four debit and credit columns across the page.[56] The methods used by masters in their disbursements were, not surprisingly, more primitive and less consistent.

Joseph's improved system of accounting after 1804 must have given him a clearer picture of the overall performance of the business. However, the accounts were still kept in such a manner as to ensure the 'books balanced' rather than to reveal the details of a vessel's performance and therefore be used as a tool of future decision-making. The reluctance of firms like Henley's to delegate authority to any great extent probably meant that there was insufficient time to analyse the accounts in greater detail as a tool of policy.[57] Instead, they would have a general notion of performance and concentrate upon finding good freights for their vessels and keeping a close watch on their masters.

Although a successful and innovative firm quick to exploit new opportunities, Henley's may not have been so advanced on the theoretical aspects of business practice. The accounts were not used as an aid to policy nor did the firm possess much idea of capital accounting, in spite of the huge amounts of fixed capital they handled. Several clerks at a time were employed but, in the main, their role appears to have been limited to entering accounts in books, adding up figures and copying letters. After about 1806 several more experienced men, often friends, were employed as clerks in order to tackle the new methods. They may have been more in the line of specialist book-keepers who were beginning to emerge under the impact of the growing size of firms.[58]

Thus one can see that Henley's developed a major ship-owning operation from what began as a modest coal and general merchanting business only a generation earlier. Doubtless, the decision to concentrate upon shipowning was borne of the high profits of this industry in wartime. Once they had built up some capital from coal merchanting they were in a position to move into shipping. The accumulation of capital and its use within the firm are instructive given the mysteries which still surround early entrepreneurs in Britain. In particular, one notes that the vessels themselves only constituted two-thirds of total fixed capital, the remainder coming largely in the form of buildings, river craft and spare ship stores. This is an area of capital formation in the industry which has been largely overlooked and may be closely associated, or at least more clearly indicated, by the new professional shipowners. In addition, the high proportion of fixed to working capital in the business is noteworthy of remark in the light of conventional wisdom.

References

1. HNL/1/47. The latter figure approximates to the amount three colliers could deliver to London in a year.
2. HNL/2/3-13.
3. HNL/8/1.
4. HNL/3/4.
5. HNL/3/3.
6. All entries from the London Directories.

7. HNL/8/4.
8. HNL/8/13.
9. Public Record Office (P.R.O.), Board of Trade 107. Though this simply followed common practice on the registers.
10. HNL/19/12.
11. HNL/19/12. Henley's never acted as shipbuilders or repairers, though as late as November 1812 Joseph was thinking about buying Howdon's Dock at South Shields. Michael was unkeen and wrote, '... there is so many new docks made at S. Shields ... that I think there is now more docks than employ for them, and my advice is to having nothing to do with it.'
12. HNL/1/8. See a forthcoming guide to the Henley Collection by Anne Currie which includes background information on the family.
13. R. Davis, *The Rise of the English Shipping Industry in the Seventeenth and Eighteenth Centuries*, London, 1962, p. 389.
14. For example, see C. H. Feinstein, 'Capital Formation in Great Britain', in P. Mathias & M. Postan (eds.), *Cambridge Economic History of Europe*, London, 1978, 7, 1, pp. 40–2.
15. A good analysis of the problems of tonnage measurement before this date can be found in C. French, 'Eighteenth century shipping tonnage measurements', *Journal of Economic History*, XXXIII, 1973, pp. 434–43. Vessels bought and sold in the same year are not included in table six and were largely used for breaking up or speculative resale.
16. HNL/19/1.
17. Feinstein, 'Capital Formation', p. 65.
18. Contemporary evidence, especially from the Henley collection and Parliamentary reports, suggests vessels depreciated most in their early years and hardly at all after the age of twenty-five or thirty. Beginning with the figure of £20 when new, it is suggested that £1 of value was lost in each of the first five years. For the following twenty years a lower rate of £1 every two years is applied. This means that a vessel was worth £5 per ton at the age of twenty-five. It is then taken to be worth £4 for the next five years and for any vessel older than this a valuation of £3 would seem appropriate. Such an index can only be an approximation but it does make it possible to measure real movements in the value of the fleet over time and moves away from the false assumption of constant depreciation.
19. These figures are taken from HNL/18/11, HNL/24/1,2,3,4,5,7,8, 10,11,12,13,14,16.
20. HNL/3/1-4.
21. HNL/4/1-13.
22. P.R.O., Admiralty (ADM) 106/1228, Navy Board Miscellaneous In – Letters 1775, E-H. Also see ADM 106/1257, Navy Board Miscellaneous In – Letters 1780, D-J.

23. HNL/3/2.
24. HNL/3/2.
25. HNL/3/2.
26. HNL/3/1,2.
27. HNL/4/3.
28. HNL/4/4.
29. HNL/4/5.
30. HNL/4/5.
31. HNL/23/5.
32. HNL/23/7.
33. HNL/23/7.
34. See HNL/6/3. Repairs were carried out on five barges in 1781.
35. See HNL/6/5. Repairs were carried out on five barges in 1783.
36. *Report from the Committee Appointed to Consider of the Coal Trade of this Kingdom*, 1800, p. 131.
37. These figures are taken from HNL/1/47,48,52,54, HNL/24/1, 7,8.
38. *Coal Trade Committee*, 1800, p. 69.
39. HNL/8/6.
40. HNL/8/1.
41. HNL/8/10.
42. HNL/8/10,11.
43. HNL/8/13.
44. HNL/8/13.
45. HNL/8/13.
46. HNL/8/13.
47. See S. Pollard, 'Fixed capital in the Industrial Revolution in Britain', *Journal of Economic History*, XXIV, 1964, pp. 299–314. He argues that with the Industrial Revolution fixed capital ratios grew as more firms adopted factory, or capital intensive, methods. The fixed capital ratio of an advanced firm need be no greater in 1830 than 1700; it was simply that there were more 'advanced' firms with these higher fixed capital ratios.
48. S. D. Chapman, *The Early Factory Masters*, Newton Abbott, 1967, p. 126.
49. See Ralph Davis, 'Maritime history: progress and problems', in S. Marriner (ed.), *Business and Businessmen*, Liverpool, 1978, pp. 178–81; D. C. North, 'Sources of productivity change in ocean shipping, 1600–1850', *Journal of Political Economy*, LXXVI, 1968, pp. 953–70; J. F. Shepherd & G. M. Walton, *Shipping, Maritime Trade and the Economic Development of Colonial North America*, Cambridge, 1972, p. 73; S. Ville, 'Total factor productivity in the English shipping industry: the north-east coal trade, 1700–1850', *Economic History Review*, 2nd series, XXXIX, 3, 1986, pp. 355–70.

50. C. H. Feinstein, 'Capital Formation in Great Britain', discusses circulating capital in the form of unsold or semi-manufactured goods, yet does not examine working capital.
51. A 'fitter' was a representative of a colliery owner whose job it was to arrange the sale of coal to shipowners when their vessels arrived in the north-east.
52. Pollard, 'Fixed Capital', p. 302.
53. S. Pollard, *The Genesis of Modern Management*, London, 1965, p. 212 is similarly pessimistic, 'even where fixed assets were used, such as houses or ships, they were not entered into the accounts, as they did not change hands during the transactions and no value could be attached to them'.
54. Davis, *English Shipping Industry*, p. 83.
55. Pollard, *Modern Management*, p. 221, agrees that an account was normally made of goods transferred from one department to another.
56. See B. S. Yamey, 'Edward Jones and the reform of book-keeping, 1795–1810', in A. C. Littleton & B. S. Yamey (eds.), *Studies in the History of Accounting*, London, 1956, pp. 313–24.
57. This tends to confirm Pollard's scepticism about the use of accounting in company policy and throw further doubt on the classical Weber-Sombart thesis which argued for the rationalisation of accounting techniques during the industrial revolution. See S. Pollard, 'Capital Accounting in the Industrial Revolution', in F. Crouzet (ed.), *Capital Formation in the Industrial Revolution*, London, 1972, pp. 119–44; M. Weber, *General Economic History*, Glencoe, 1958 and W. Sombart, *The Quintessence of Capitalism: A Study of the History and Psychology of the Modern Businessman*, London, 1915.
58. N. A. H. Stacey, *English Accountancy, 1800–1954*, London, 1954, pp. 16–18.

H.C. Moses   A. West India

3 · Ships – construction, exchange and deployment

in Cox & Curlins yard Limehouse

National shipping statistics for the late eighteenth and nineteenth centuries deal largely with aggregates such as the number of vessels built each year or the tonnage entered and cleared from particular ports.[1] These figures tell us nothing of the individual ship, her construction, lifespan or employment. The statutory shipping registers from 1786 are more helpful.[2] They detail a vessel's date and place of build along with her general dimensions and subsequent fate. The shipping registers, though, give no idea of the cargo capacity of a vessel, this 'tons burthen' being the critical figure for shipowners. Studying the papers of an individual firm gives a clearer impression of the general construction features of a vessel, the market in ships and the manner of their deployment. The Henley experience is especially instructive because of the large number of prizes which they owned, enabling a comparison between British and foreign tonnage. Moreover, the French Wars accentuated cyclical trends in the market for ships and initiated several major changes in the patterns of deployment. The firm's response to such uncertainties is of much interest.

Construction

By the middle of the eighteenth century the north-east of England 'was by far the largest seat of the shipbuilding industry' with Whitby and Scarborough built ships having particular reputations for great stowage and cheap operation.[3] By 1776 around 40% of English tonnage was launched in the north-east.[4] Low construction costs and sound design established it as a major centre of shipbuilding. These conclusions are confirmed by Henley's experience. Thirty-three of their vessels were prizes, thirty-seven were built in the North-East (north of the Wash), thirteen in the South-East, including five in the Thames, and fourteen spread around the west of England, including three at both Liverpool and Newhaven. A further three were British built vessels that had been recaptured or bought from neutrals. One vessel was built in each of Newfoundland, Quebec, Nova Scotia and Greenock. One vessel was Swedish built and was partially reconstructed for Henley's after her previous owner had abandoned her on the Goodwin sands. The reliance on the north-east coast is particularly marked among vessels kept by Henley's for at least five years

Table 7. *Place of construction of principal vessels*

Place of construction	Ships[a]		Average size
Whitby	7	(2,519)	360
Stockton	3	(772)	257
North Shields	2	(659)	330
Gainsborough	2	(633)	317
Scarborough	2	(544)	272
Liverpool	1	(465)	465
Hull	1	(347)	347
Thames	1	(324)	324
North Yarmouth	1	(319)	319
Sweden	1	(247)	247
Whitehaven	1	(242)	242
Prizes			
Country unknown	3	(690)	230
France	1	(553)	553
Denmark	2	(472)	236
Netherlands	1	(358)	358

Note (a) Tonnage in brackets.

(Table 7). Seventeen out of twenty-nine such vessels were built in the North-East, principally at Whitby.[5] Despite the large amount of shipbuilding on the Thames, about 20% of the national figure, Henley's only kept one London ship for more than five years. Seven prizes were also retained either because they were of a suitable design or were cheap enough to permit cost effective repairs.

Henley's preference for north-east vessels also reflected their coal trade interests where cargo capacity and durability were essential. With the exception of the Baltic, the trades of northern Europe were not seasonal, so speed was less important. North-east vessels were very flat bottomed which gave them a large cargo capacity. Henley's *Telemachus*, built at Newcastle, had a cargo capacity 77% larger than her measured tonnage and the *Ann*, from Gainsborough, was 75% larger. On average, their vessels from the north-east had a capacity-tonnage differential of 54%. On the west coast it was only 22%. The differential was

47% for all of their British vessels. The variety of constructions is illustrated by a standard deviation of seventeen percentage points around this figure.

Many dues were levied according to measured or registered tonnage and so shipowners wished to minimise payments while maximising capacity. Convoys slowed down shipping movements for much of this period so that fine-hulled vessels with smaller holds though capable of travelling faster were of little use.[6] The *Neptune* had a differential of only 19% and was kept for just a year. *Peggy* and *Aurora* faced a similar fate. All three vessels were built in the United States where lower tidal ranges made fine-hulled vessels more suitable. However, the *Ocean*, also American, was described as a 'sharp' ship and yet had a differential of 60%. The *Adelphi* from Quebec had a differential of 32% in contrast to the 55% of the *Valiant* from Newfoundland. Fine-hulled vessels in America may explain the lower capacities of vessels on the west coast of Britain. The *Trusty* from Liverpool had a capacity only 5% larger than her measurements and the *Europa* of Bristol only 10%. European prizes generally carried less than British vessels though the *Fame*, a Danish prize, had a capacity 73% greater than her dimensions. In 1813 M. Alexander of Bristol wrote to Henley's saying, 'we needn't tell you that Danish built vessels are not much approved of tho' the *Fame* appears to be a good strong vessel and certainly burthen a large cargo for her tonnage.'[7]

Flat bottomed vessels could use bar harbours more easily, remain afloat in shallow water and use berths that dried out at low water. This was useful for loading colliers at staiths on the Tyne. In discharging coal for the Navy Board a similar problem existed: 'The vessel [Ocean] being a sharp ship and cannot be laid on the ground we pray an order may be sent to the respective officers at Plymouth to deliver the vessel at the North Jetty where she will lay afloat'.[8] The request was rejected by the Navy Board. Sharp-hulled vessels often had to discharge with the aid of lighters nor could they be repaired on dry ground, 'we may as well heave the money into the river hear as repair her on the ways', captain Weakner remarked of the *Nancy* in 1811.[9] It was easier to sell older ships which could be inspected on dry ground. Flat vessels were more suited to the stowage of awkwardly shaped goods. Captain Dodds observed of a vessel for sale at Portsmouth:

'she apears to be flat from forit to the main mast but from thence aft she is varey sharp which would be much against hur stowing masts ... she would make onley an unhandy collier and would not answer to lay on shore load she appears to be a well bult dutch ship.'[10]

Other construction features were important. *Adelphi* had a small capacity yet sailed slowly, causing captain Atkinson to exclaim, 'she are not a good sailer – all I can do she will not keep up with the convoys on account of her main mast being so far forward'.[11] James Kirton had advised the removal of the mizzen mast of the *Nancy* so that she would be lighter aloft and sail more easily without ballast.[12] Sailing without ballast was important for colliers because its continual loading and discharge was expensive and time consuming. The inability of the *George* to sail without ballast was 'a troublesome and expensive business'.[13] If a vessel was too heavy in her bottom, sometimes through incorrect loading, she would labour; if too heavy aloft, she would not grip the water sufficiently, making ballast necessary. In January 1814, Captain Watson took on thirty or forty tons of ballast, 'as the *Trusty* is very crank'.[14] Vessels were often two-masted in the coal trade which made them less heavy aloft, reduced manning and facilitated access to the cargo hatches. Thus one finds some large two-masted vessels such as Henley's *Pitt* of 330 tons and *Oeconomy* of 365 tons which were both snows, whilst *Zephyr* of 400 tons was converted from a ship to a snow and back to a ship once more.[15]

The use of copper sheathing was growing, especially in the transport service, where coppered vessels were paid a higher freight rate and owners sought to protect their vessels against 'worming' during long delays in the Mediterranean.[16] Henley's generally sheathed their vessels before offering them to the government for long service.

Shipbuilding remained a matter of craftmanship where individuals could develop reputations and considerable judgement and risk were involved in the purchase of a vessel. Suspicion surrounded the use of ephemeral American timber in the internal structure of some ships. Structural weaknesses in the *Harry Morris* were revealed by her master, 'her stern frame is weak and in my opinion she makes all the water in the consequence of it – when at sea she is like an electrifying machine'.[17] The sailing qualities of a vessel could vary over time. In January 1819, captain Haden of the *Star* noted, 'I fear her rolling is a natural disorder and will require more than common abilities to cure – she played some pretty tunes in the Downs'. Eighteen months later his report was very different, 'the old lady sails like a witch and has gained great credit by her good behaviour she is as easy as an old shoe this voyage'.[18] Poor stowage was the problem with the *Pitt*, 'I never seed so much alterations in a ship ... she will neither sail or anything else and I cannot acct for it without it be the cargo she's in'.[19]

At least one Henley vessel, *Cornwall*, was a former ship of war. She was a bomb vessel bought from the Navy Board in 1810 and proved so valuable that she was retained for two decades.[20] Henley's made an abortive offer for a sloop and attended the sale of many naval vessels. This renders questionable the belief that by about 1715, 'the divorce between ships of war and commerce was complete'.[21] Henley's naturally preferred merchant vessels but would consider buying a cheap naval ship and converting her. After 1815 many naval vessels were sold for only a pound or two per ton which deepened the shipbuilding depression.[22]

Henley's preferred medium-sized vessels between about 200 and 400 tons which were suitable for use in many trades. The average size of vessels they employed was 263 tons, two-thirds of which fell within this band.[23] Of vessels kept for at least five years, more than three-quarters came within the 200–400 range, none were less than 100 tons and the average size was 315 tons. Average size grew from 308 tons in the 1790s to 325 two decades later (five-year vessels). The former figure would have been 285 without the inclusion of the *General Elliot* of 553 tons. This growth over time was due to the purchase of five larger vessels of around 400 tons for use in the Canadian timber trade and a temporary movement away from the coal and Baltic trades where many bar harbours prohibited larger vessels. Their suspicion of smaller vessels was expressed in a letter from K. Izod in 1788, 'you'd doe well to be rid of her, small vessells are in general but pick pockets'.[24]

The longest period Henley's owned a vessel was forty years in the case of *Freedom* and thirty-one years with *Henley*. The average length of ownership was 4·2 years, though this has been depressed by ships captured or bought for speculative resale.

Table 8. *Average size of vessels*

Tonnage range	1-100	101-200	201-300	301-400	401-500	501-600
Number (and %) of vessels	4(5)	19(21)	37(41)	26(29)	3(3)	1(1)

The growth in the length of ownership after 1790, in spite of war, reflects Henley's increasing concentration on shipowning. It is also indicative of the problems shipowners faced in procuring new tonnage in wartime and therefore chose to retain existing vessels. The length of ownership also rose in the firm's twilight years as a few old vessels were simply retained. Not surprisingly, the medium-sized vessels were kept the longest.

Table 9. *Average length of ownership of vessels*

Tonnage	1780s	1790s	1800s	1810s	1820s
Average:	3·7	8·8	6·1	6·7	15·8
1-100	1·0	0	1·0	0	0
101-200	10·0	7·8	3·8	3·1	0
201-300	4·5	4·9	4·6	4·0	10·0
301-400	4·5	16·9	12·5	9·6	19·3
401-500	6·0	6·0	0	9·5	9·5
501-600	6·0	6·0	0	0	0

Henley's bought only one new vessel throughout the French Wars, the *Lord Nelson*, which was only secured after many abortive enquiries to shipbuilders along the north-east coast at Whitby, Scarborough, Bridlington, Hull, Gainsborough, Selby, Thorne, Stockwith and Stockton and also at Heath, Milford, Dover and Lynn.[25] Shipbuilders had orders for years to come and were not interested in any more. Therefore, Henley's bought in the second-hand market and concentrated on maintaining existing vessels as long as possible. This necessitated careful maintenance and repair of an ageing fleet. Doubtless, many other owners took a similar attitude and so it is not surprising to find

Kirton writing to Henley's in December 1809, 'I never seed so much to dow in docking ships as theres at present wheres theres one vacant theres five ships for it.'[26] Thomas Barnes, a ship-owner, pointed out another advantage to operating old vessels in wartime: 'the premium of insurance on a small sum is less than that on a greater sum, the premium being in time of war larger than in time of peace, merchants go to sea on the smallest capital they can, therefore they give preference to the ship of the smallest value'.[27]

By 1810 Henley's began to think about buying newer vessels. Joseph wrote, 'we do not intend to keep her [*Oeconomy*] longer than new ships are to be had you see how we are sett fast with the *Pitt* and *Norfolk* their is no getting them to sea when loaded on account their depth'.[28] These vessels were too crank and leaky and Henley's realised new vessels would be easier to find as war drew to a close. In December 1812 Michael was pleased that *London* was sold, 'I should have no objection to the *Zepher* being the same, and all the old ships, I agree with you new ships is best for us'.[29] This did not work out in practice; after 1810 the average age of new acquisitions was twenty. In the last few war years Henley's changed their mind; with the growing depression and the reversion back to the bulk trades, they persisted with older vessels. *Peggy* was fifty-six when bought in 1816. Thomas Rooke, judging her condition for Henley's observed, 'McGhie, Beatson & Co had the *Peggy* in dock here three years ago they declare she opned better than many ships only seven years old'.[30]

In 1821 Joseph Henley reflected, 'such constructed ships as *Peggy* are always valuable in the worst of times for the timber and coal trades ... the age for timber and coals we never think of'.[31] This confirms that Henley's use of older vessels was due to their interests in coal and timber as well as because of war. Moreover, the lifespan of a vessel was probably longer than historians have assumed. Davis believed vessels had a depreciation rate of 4 or 5% per annum[32] and that twenty-five years would probably see the end of their profitable and safe use in distant trades with cargoes of substantial value.[33] By this age their structure would have weakened a good deal. Kirton had noted, 'when they excead the years of 20 it is rather precarious to brick into them for repairs'.[34] However, vessels could be employed for many years in the coal and timber trades where bulky cargoes meant a high demand for shipping. Abel Chapman, a shipowner, knew of a 400 ton vessel which lasted nearly sixty years and believed that vessels would last 'for ever' if kept in a good state of repair.[35] George Norman, a timber merchant, estimated the average age of ships in the Norway to England timber trade as forty years, 'it arises from the nature of the cargo they carry ... old ships that can just keep together and swim will do'.[36] Older vessels also tended to depreciate more slowly.[37]

Long periods serving as a transport reduced a vessel's lifespan because of dangerous and unpredictable work. Kirton once noted, 'ships in the service appears to be a sinking fund, likewise the ship must decrease in value much'.[38] It was estimated in 1813 that the natural life of a transport was twenty-four years.[39] In general, the average lifespan of a vessel was in excess of thirty years with the potential, if well built and properly maintained, of lasting much longer.

Exchange

Various estimates have been made of the price of a ton shipping at the end of the eighteenth century ranging from around £5 up to £20.[40] Thomas Gillespy, a coal factor and shipowner, remarked of the cost of a collier, 'it varies according to peace or war, and wether the ships are old or new. On average, I think in peaceable times about £5 per ton; at present £10.'[41] Prices also varied according to a vessel's age, her general condition, the state of her stores and where and by whom she had been built all of which makes it difficult to estimate accurately the changing value of shipping, especially second hand.

The outbreak of war in 1793 led to a rise in ship prices as the government expanded the number of active naval vessels and ordered the chartering of transports. Experienced shipowners, like Michael Henley, conscious of previous wartime booms, began to invest in new shipping. Of only four vessels which Henley's bought new, two were completed in 1791 and one in 1792. When they were taking tenders for the construction of *Freedom* in 1791, a builder from Shoreham, Edwards, offered to build for £2,175. Michael Henley replied that this was £500 too much only to be rebuked by Edwards that this was cheap because he was using good materials and if war broke out ship prices would rise.[42] She was built at Stockton for the lower price of £5 per ton (about £1,650). The two other vessels built new for them at this time, *Ann* and *Pitt*, cost the same.[43] The *Lord Nelson*, bought new by Henley's in 1799, cost £8, which suggests prices rose about 60% in the 1790s, although prices varied between builders. Tenders for *Lord Nelson* varied from £6 per ton in Stockton to £9 in Lynn.[44]

Less is known of prices of new vessels during the Napoleonic phase of the wars. In 1812 a new vessel of 223 tons was for sale at £10 per ton and in 1814 a 326 ton vessel was offered at £20, both at Shields.[45] In 1816 a new Sunderland vessel was for sale at £9 12s and in 1819 a new Bristol vessel was offered at £12 or £13.[46] After 1815 prices and demand fell; Thames built vessels which had fetched £26 during the war were offered at £15 'and less would no doubt be taken'.[47] Many believed that the state of shipbuilding was worse than during the post-war declines of 1782 and 1802 because costs remained high.[48] Michael remarked as early as 1811 that demand was on the decline and 'shipbuilders will injure themselves for every one has a ship on at every hole and corner'.[49] Thomas Hall of Hull was pessimistic about getting a reasonable sale price for Henley's vessel, *Valiant*, in 1812.[50] Though by 1813 vessels were in demand at Shields because of losses incurred in the American conflict. Nor was the downturn confined to Britain, at Amsterdam 'ships are selling here for little or nothing, their coming from all quarters for sale'.[51]

An impressionistic analysis of the Henley material on second-hand vessels suggests that prices rose steadily in the 1790s. In 1792 Henley's sold the eight-year-old *Holderness* for £4 per ton and in 1798 the five-year-old *Telemachus* for £10.[52] In the first seven or eight years of the new century, second-hand prices remained fairly stable. From about 1809 they began to rise once more so that in 1811 Henley's bought *Anna* of eight years for £17.[53] Prices fell at the end of the war though they still paid £12 in 1819 for a four-year-old vessel built on the Tyne.[54] In 1824 Henley's sold four old vessels at between £5 and £7 per ton.[55]

Second-hand prices fell only slowly after 1815 because many shipowners hung on to their investments, rather than sell at a reduced value, in the hope that shipping would improve. Many

owners were unsuited to, or uninterested in, alternative investments and in some ports there were few opportunities in other
industries. However, as shipbuilders continued to build through
the depression and operate unsold vessels themselves, the second
hand market flooded and bankruptcies occurred.

Gayer, Rostow and Schwartz saw a time lag between the
general trade cycle and that for shipbuilding because of the
industry's long gestation period.[56] However, the gestation
period for most mercantile vessels was quite short, only six to
nine months, though a time lag did exist because shipbuilders
were not very responsive to trade cycles, building on speculation
in the hope that things would come good again. For this reason
there would be a time lag on the upturn of the cycle as shipbuilders unloaded their present stocks and inelastic supply conditions prevented them building many more vessels immediately.

The main influence on ship prices at this time was the course
of the French Wars. The growth of the transport service increased
the demand for ships, causing owners like Henley's to buy vessels
specifically for this use which promised long-term employment.
On the supply side, the Continental Blockade, coupled with increased import duties, raised the price and restricted the flow of
timber. In 1806 the price of Memel timber rose from 15s to over
£7 per load and to £16 by 1809.[57] Only 333 great masts were
imported from Riga and St Petersburg in 1809–10 in contrast
to 17,000 in 1807.[58] Although Baltic timber was eventually
replaced by Canadian, this could not be achieved immediately
due to the higher freight rate and absence of suitable infrastructure. In these later war years, as supply costs were rising,
the demand for shipping declined, causing captain Omond to
observe, 'ships are as hay [high] in vellow [value] as evr and you
sea ther is littel for them to do'.[59]

The number of vessels lost and gained through wartime
capture affected their price. More vessels were probably lost than
gained. Between 1793 and 1802 over 3,000 vessels were lost in
return for little more than 2,000 prizes added to the British
registers.[60] The estimated annual net loss by capture during the
Revolutionary Wars was estimated as two per cent with marine
risks nearly as high as this.[61] Henley's suffered losses by marine
risks of 2·4% and 2·5% respectively during the Revolutionary
and Napoleonic phases of the war. However, their losses by

capture were 7·1% and 2·0% respectively. Between 1795 and 1797 alone they lost five vessels from a fleet of only eleven which may explain why they paid 60% more for a new vessel in 1799 than they had in 1792. Of ten Henley vessels captured, eight had been deployed in the overseas and just two in the coasting trades, though it was not unusual for foreign-going ships to be captured while in English coastal waters. Masters often sailed without convoys in the coastal trade which may have caused a place like Shields, with most of its shipping in coasting, to suffer severe losses. Losses were also high in the Mediterranean. Henley's lost two vessels in March 1795 returning from Tenerife; the one occasion when a joint charterparty worked against Henley's by concentrating their risks.

A vessel which proved well suited to her owner's needs and yielded good profits would be difficult to replace if lost. Time was spent salvaging the vessel, dealing with insurance and looking for another vessel. When *Eagle* was lost in 1802, William Dodds, who was part owner with Henley's, remarked that in spite of her being insured, 'this shall not prevent me making yous of evrey means to save the *Eagle* she is a desireable ship and cannot be well replased'.[62]

Seasonal considerations affected the ship market. In December 1818, Kirton had problems selling the *Mary Ann* for Henley's because of the unfavourable state of the coal trade, 'and two or three winter months coming on'.[63] Nor was summer necessarily the best time to sell. In June 1811 Kirton wrote, 'had it been about three months souner that American voyage could be got I make not any doubt but the *Salus* might obtain your price'.[64] A vessel intended for the Baltic would be sold in about March or April, one for the coal trade about March to September and one for the West Indies probably in September or October, though these calculations could vary from year to year. Additional complications in wartime were the incidence of losses and the sale of prizes.

Henley's bought and sold most of their vessels on the Thames and the Tyne. Many prizes were bought from the Navy Board in London suggesting some advantages of being based in the capital. Most other vessels were bought from London or Newcastle merchants though one was purchased from a Gloucester banker, another from a Liverpool merchant, a third from a Lothian shipbuilder and another from two Guernsey merchants. Several vessels were bought from bankrupts including the *Albion* for only £350 in March 1793. She was sold in the August for £1,180 after repairs of less than £100, indicating a profit of £700.[65] Probably they paid less than the vessel's full value to the desperate bankrupt. Moreover, Michael's experience enabled him to speculate by buying on a low market at the outbreak of war and selling on a rising one some months later. This attitude led Henley's frequently to test the state of the ship market in Shields by putting a vessel up for sale at a particular price. If they received an offer at this price she would be sold, if not, she was loaded with coal and sent back to London. This 'testing' represented a flexible form of speculation. The *Lady Juliana* was offered for sale at Shields at £2,000 in September 1792, at £1,450 in March 1803, at £4,000 in November 1813 and £2,400 in January 1816.[66] Most vessels were sold to London or Tyneside merchants though the exceptions included owners from Margate, Chepstow and Montrose. These sales were either arranged through business contacts or by putting a vessel up for sale when visiting ports. Moreover, owners came to Newcastle from nearby ports like Hull and Whitby, but also Scotland, aware of the port's thriving ship market.

Henley's concentrated the purchase and sale of vessels into particular years. Most purchases occurred in 1788–93, 1803–6, 1808–11 and 1816. Sales were concentrated into the years 1789–91, 1810–14 and 1824. Henley's bought vessels on the eve of war, in expectation of a rising market, and sold towards the end of the war, fearing a depression. The fact that they bought many ships before the outbreak of war and sold them again before the end of hostilities suggests they anticipated the market well. They also bought groups of vessels when the Navy Board auctioned prizes or if the demand for transports was high.

Henley's relied heavily upon auctions to buy and sell vessels, notice of which would be advertised in local newspapers and on handbills. They also followed the contemporary practice of placing a broom across the bows to indicate that she was for sale. Kirton played an important part in selling many vessels for Henley's at good prices on the Tyne. As an experienced ship master and owner he was familiar with the local ship market and was able to judge which vessels would sell profitably. His ability to strike a hard bargain is illustrated by the sale of *Europa* in

March 1813. He insisted on taking no less than £1,400 for her. The potential buyer refused to pay this price and returned to his home in Whitby. Several days later, after consulting his friends, he agreed to pay Kirton's price.[67] In the same year, Kirton advised against trying to sell the *Alice* at Shields, saying that her great length and tendency to touch the ground would make it difficult to find a buyer. He was proved correct when nobody turned up for the auction.[68] Similarly, in March 1811 he wrote that the *Adelphi* would not sell well since she was too deep and narrow for the coal trade and would require ballast.[69]

As well as selling many of their vessels, Kirton kept Henley's informed about shipbuilding and repairs, such as in June 1812 when various ships were being built on the Tyne and several were nearing completion.[70] He arranged dock facilities for their vessels and once compared the standard of sheathing in London and the north-east, 'I must give the prefference to Shields ... they take more pains to putt it on and likewise calkes it better ... cheaper at London'.[71]

Deployment

Henley's deployed their vessels in a flexible and intensive manner especially during the French Wars, the outbreak of which encouraged them to diversify into many trades rather than concentrate on the coal trade as they had in the 1770s and 1780s.[72] New opportunities appeared particularly in the transport service and the Atlantic trades, though this must be set against the temporary closure of the French and Baltic markets. Given the scissors movement in the supply and demand for shipping during wartime, Henley's were able to keep their vessels at sea for most of the time. After 1815, the position was reversed and their vessels were frequently laid up or confined to a limited number of trades.

Normally, Henley's arranged freights for their vessels before they sailed, by signing a charterparty with the merchant which generally guaranteed a full cargo. Joseph was a member of Lloyds and held influence within the London mercantile community which enabled him to secure diverse and regular employment for a large fleet. Occasionally, they worked through brokers though this was a last option only used extensively in the final years of the business when Joseph was in semi-retirement. Only in times of depression would they send their vessels out in search of freights and even then they had to be reasonably hopeful of success. Often they signed agreements for several or more of their vessels simultaneously to freight a merchant's goods. This was a mutually beneficial arrangement. It saved the merchant time by dealing with only one shipowner. For Henley's it put them in a stronger bargaining position than a smaller owner, it enabled them to find employment for several vessels simultaneously and to bypass brokers. In addition, the firm yielded a wide range of economies by having several vessels doing the same work, especially in terms of administration and voyage costs. Vessels could also help each other out if problems arose.

We know little of the Henley fleet's deployment before 1790 though it appears most vessels were confined to the coal trade with occasional forays into the transport service. The *Henley*, for example, worked in the coal trade from 1775 to 1791 except for a brief period as a transport in 1782–3. In discussing deployment more systematically from 1790, nine geographical areas can be distinguished namely coasting, Northern Europe (including the North Sea and the Baltic), France, the Mediterranean (including Spain and Portugal), the East, North America, Central America, the West Indies and South America. One half of vessels owned for three years or more had voyaged to at least four of these areas. Looking at the principal twelve vessels owned for at least a decade shows that 75% had been flexibly deployed in four or more trades (see Table 10).

Most of these dozen vessels were of a handy medium size between 200 and 400 tons.[73] *Henley*, the smallest vessel, spent much of her time in the coasting trade, whilst *Trusty*, the largest, made only one such voyage. Most of them were built in the reputable yards of the North-East and four, *Lord Nelson*, *Pitt*, *Ann* and *Freedom*, were the only vessels bought new by the firm and were designed with Henley's deployment policies in mind. They were suitable for work in a wide range of trades so long as their general condition did not preclude them from the carriage of valuable or easily damaged goods. Many of their vessels were old but maintained in a good condition. Thus *Freedom* was still in the West Indies trade when she was twenty-four years old.[74] The existence of many printed guides to stowage, with their freight rate conversion tables from one cargo to another, enabled many

Table 10.   *Trades in which main twelve vessels were deployed,*
1790–1830

Vessel	Tonnage	Coastal	Baltic	Medit.	W. Inds.	Honduras	S. Am.	N. Am.	Fran.	East
Ann	243	×	×	×					×	
Cornwall	368	×	×		×	×		×		
Freedom	317	×	×	×	×	×	×	×		
Friendship	225	×	×	⊗						
Heart of Oak	324	×	×	⊗						⊗
Henley	181	×	×					⊗		
Lady Juliana	379	×	×	⊗	⊗	×		×	⊗	
Lord Nelson	319	×	×	⊗	×	×	⊗	×		⊗
Norfolk	319	×	×	⊗						
Pitt	291	×	×	⊗					×	
Polly	285	×	×	⊗			⊗	×		
Trusty	465	×	×		×	×		×		

Note ○ = Deployment in transport service only.

different commodities to be carried on the same vessel.[75] *Freedom* carried many different cargoes from valuable colonial produce like rum, sugar and coffee, to government stores, troops, timber and coal.

Far from there being ship specialisation in particular trades, it was the master who was likely to be committed to a specific area. He would familiarise himself with the navigational problems and build up commercial contacts. The existence of vertical integration of merchant and shipowner explains the preference of some owners for a particular trade. This is why Henley's deployed most of their vessels in the coal trade in the early years when they were primarily merchants.

Henley vessels were rarely laid up in wartime. Only during the temporary peace of 1801–3 and from the final years of the French Wars were they idle for more than 10% of the time. The end of the war meant a lower demand for shipping, especially as transports, and an expanded effective supply with the end of the convoy system. After 1815 vessels made more passages in ballast as they went searching for freights.

The intensive use of the Henley fleet in wartime suggests high productivity because vessels were more fully employed and therefore frequently completed more voyages than in peacetime. Given that certain inputs such as depreciation, entrepreneurial costs and some wages were incurred irrespective of whether the vessel was employed or idle, productivity rose. On the other hand, the convoy system lengthened times and therefore increased costs. Ballast passages were kept to a minimum by prearranged charterparties. However, most of Henley's work remained in the import trades and therefore some unladen passages were unavoidable. The coal and timber trades remained largely one-way although sometimes coal was exported to northern Europe or naval bases in the Mediterranean and Henley's vessels managed to secure a return freight. Vessels bringing back colonial produce from the West Indies sometimes took government stores on the outward passage though never a full cargo. Nor was there ever any attempt to combine this with African trading. Vessels sailed for the West Indies before the size of the sugar or coffee harvest was known; a shortfall would make it difficult to secure a full cargo. In the war years when vessels were in demand, Henley's normally had a clause inserted into charterparties guaranteeing the payment of 'dead freight' by the merchant on unutilised cargo space. Though in the shipping depression after 1815 it was normally the shipowner who had to stand the loss of returning half laden. It was as transports that the capacity of Henley vessels was most effectively utilised, generally sailing fully laden. On the other hand, transports were often used as 'floating warehouses', suggesting an inefficient use of valuable shipping capital. In the coal trade productivity rose as vessels completed more voyages, unhampered by convoys, and infrastructure improvements took place, especially in the methods of loading coal at Newcastle although losses were probably quite high. In the long hauls fewer voyages were completed because convoys were infrequent and took a long time to organise. From 1798 convoys were compulsory for most foreign-going vessels although Henley's managed to get licences for their larger vessels to sail alone but at the cost of higher insurance.

Coasting was for long Henley's most important area of deployment. It was the origin and backbone of the business, steadying it during the years of expansion. This suggests, assuming an interest from other owners, the large size of London's coastal traffic which remains largely unrecorded in national returns.[76] Mostly Henley's delivered Newcastle coal to London and the dockyards of Woolwich, Chatham, Sheerness, Portsmouth and Plymouth. There were a few voyages to Ireland in the early years though further deployment here was discouraged by the reports of Captain Dann of the *Polly* that the Irish were guilty of greediness, drunkenness and cheating.[77]

The coal trade was regarded by the firm as a normal or shuttle service from which vessels would be removed when better opportunities appeared in other trades.[78] It offered many benefits including a reliable rate of return and contact with the valuable market in ships and their repair on the north-east coast. A voyage or two to Newcastle filled in periods of idleness for vessels in the seasonal long hauls and they could be repaired there, partly financed by the profits of such a voyage. By keeping a regular supply of vessels in the coal trade it enabled them to gain some economies of scale; suppliers of coal and provisions vied for their patronage. The firm supplied coal to the dockyards under contracts which required them to provide a specified amount of coal over a certain period of time. This offered the benefit of some guaranteed future employment whilst facilitating flexibility in the firm's deployment policies. Henley's sometimes freighted vessels belonging to other owners to deliver at the dockyards if their own vessels were more profitably employed elsewhere or if the remaining amounts on the contract were too small for their own vessels to carry economically. After about 1803 fewer of their vessels went to the dockyards following a revelation that their ships had been recording a larger delivery of coal than was legitimate as a result of bribing the officials of Plymouth yard.[79] In the later years of the French Wars fewer Henley vessels delivered coal at London so that by 1813, with falling coal prices, Joseph Henley exclaimed, 'I do not intend to have anything to do with colliers for some time to come'.[80] The trade continued in an unprofitable state for some years; in 1822 James Kirton noted, 'to go in the coal trade it's dowing worse than nothing'.[81]

Henley vessels spent a disproportionate amount of time in the transport service, up to 60% or 70%, compared with the national figure of 8% to 10% of the British merchant fleet. This may have been one of the respects by which embryonic shipowners availed themselves of the opportunities presented by war. The first boom in transport activity, in the mid-1790s, took Henley vessels to the campaign in the West Indies. The emphasis then switched to the Mediterranean at the turn of the nineteenth century and also to the Baltic by 1805–6. In the following years Henley transports went to South America, as a result of conflict with

Argentina, and to the Cape of Good Hope and India, before returning to the Mediterranean in 1809–11.

Most Henley shipping in the North Sea and Baltic was concerned with coal, timber and other shipbuilding materials, along with a small amount of re-exported West Indian produce, trading principally with Amsterdam, Cronstadt, Memel, Archangel, Christiania and Riga. The Continental Blockade, together with the timber duties of 1806 and 1811[82] and the emergence of the Canadian timber trade, all served to make the demand for shipping in the Baltic highly volatile. With the decline in the demand for shipbuilding materials after 1815, Henley vessels wasted many ballast passages searching for freights. By 1819 the post-war optimism about the future of the Baltic timber trade had collapsed,[83] though the narrowing of the duty differential between Canadian and Baltic timber in 1821, together with improved trading conditions, explain Henley deployment here in the mid 1820s.

The growth of the North American timber trade is one of the main features of this period. No Henley vessels traded with Canada until 1808 and it did not become a central policy of the business until 1817, when it replaced the fruitless post-war ventures into the Baltic. Mostly their vessels loaded at Quebec though some also at Miramichi, St John's (New Brunswick), Pictou and Pugwash in spite of early misgivings when currency, provisions and a sufficient depth of water were hard to come by and discount and commission on bills high. Captain Darley reported in 1815 that most vessels had to wait six or seven weeks for a good tide.[84] However, once the infrastructure was improved it became the natural alternative for larger vessels discharged from the transport service and unable to find profitable employment in the Baltic.

A quadrupling of freight rates in the Honduras to London mahogany trade induced Henley's to enter into this risky area as a suitable counterbalance against the more reliable though less profitable coastal and short sea trades. Amongst the risks associated with the Honduras trade were the proximity of Belize to Spanish settlements and the unpredictability of the climate and terrain. In 1819 the *Trusty* was delayed four months for lack of water in the river by which to float the wood down to the harbour for loading.[85] At the end of the French Wars freight rates collapsed and alternative sources of furnishing wood were developed in Africa, Jamaica, British Guiana, New Zealand and India.

Deployment in the West Indies was similarly encouraged by high wartime freight rates. Captain Robson of the *Concord* noted during a transport voyage to the West Indies in 1794–6 that as much money could be made from a passage home with a freight of produce as could be earned in twelve months as a transport.[86] Henley vessels brought sugar, coffee, rum, cocoa and cotton back to London from the existing British colonies of St Vincents, Jamaica and St Kitts rather than go to newly gained colonies like St Lucia and Trinidad. In South America they were quicker to 'follow the flag', voyaging to Surinam, Berbice and Demerara from 1806. This reflected British attempts to fill the 'maritime and commercial vacuum'[87] resulting from a series of revolutions in Latin America. This explains why no Henley vessels went to the West Indies between 1805 and 1809. At the end of the war they returned here to face an over capacity of shipping in the area.

After 1815 not only was it more difficult to find work for the firm's fleet but there was a contraction of their activities into only the coal and timber trades. From conducting a tramp style operation during the French Wars, suited to the rapidly changing conditions, they now reverted to a more liner fashion, remaining constantly in just a few trades. This reflected the absence of opportunities for innovative policies in these depressed years together with the lack of dynamism in the business with Joseph ageing and no heir apparent. There was a temporary revival in the mid 1820s when their vessels were kept busy but Joseph's response was to sell up most of his fleet on this high market.

Henley's deployment policies did not always match national trends.[88] At the outbreak of war in 1793, most of their foreign-going shipping was trading in the North Sea and Baltic. Nationally, this was also the largest area of shipping flows. No figures exist for coasting before the end of the French Wars. Nearly a fifth of national entrances were from Ireland, an area where Henley's possessed no interest. By 1803, most national entrances still related to northern Europe and Ireland. However, Henley's Baltic voyages were now being surpassed, if temporarily, by ventures to the West Indies. Over the next few years Henley's expansion into the Atlantic trades far outstripped national growth in this area. Honduras, for example, occupied up to a quarter of Henley's time but never constituted more than 1% of national entrances at this time. The firm's movement into the Canadian timber trade from 1808 closely mirrors the national trend. These national comparisons demonstrate more clearly Henley's rapid response to the opportunities of wartime which enabled them to concentrate upon shipowning.

The pattern that emerges as the Henley business develops is of an increasing concentration on those trades where merchants were less likely to provide the vessels required, particularly the transport service and the Atlantic trades. This created an opening for the specialist. Whaling has also been identified as suitable for the emerging specialist. Again this trade was not so clearly connected with merchanting and its nature allowed the use of old, cheap vessels by shipowners who would move into or out of the trade according to market conditions.[89] Henley's, though, never became involved in whaling.

One can see that Henley's favoured old, medium-sized vessels built in the reputable shipbuilding centres along the north-east coast. These vessels were easier to obtain than new ones, especially in wartime, facilitated cheap operation, were suitable for a wide range of deployment and possessed a reputation for sturdiness, capacity and longevity. Failing this, they were prepared to buy cheap prizes either for speculative resale or genuine employment. A third of their fleet was prizes which has enabled comparisons between British and foreign shipbuilding, particularly the tendency of the latter to be more fine-hulled and of smaller carrying capacity. It is also clear that more flexible terms of reference are required when talking about brigs, snows, ships and barques since many were converted from one kind of rig to another with comparative ease. Most Henley vessels were bought and sold in London and Newcastle, in the latter under the guidance of their Shields agent, James Kirton. The price and availability of vessels fluctuated rapidly under the changing conditions of war and peace but, in general, their experience and expertise enabled Henley's to play the market quite successfully, buying vessels on a low market on the eve of war and selling out towards the end of hostilities before prices collapsed. The manner in which the vessels were employed was similarly influenced by wartime conditions, with the temporary closure of some of the

Table 11. *Distribution of deployment, 1790–1830 (%)*

Year	Laid up	Coast	Baltic	Medit.	W. Inds.	N. Am.	Hond.	S. Am.	France	East	Total ship yrs.	Prop. of active employment spent in tran. ser.
1790	7	56	6	7	16	0	8	0	0	0	9	32
1791	2	72	16	0	0	0	8	0	2	0	8·3	12
1792	3	54	38	5	0	0	0	0	0	0	8·6	18
1793	0	70	21	4	5	0	0	0	0	0	8·3	29
1794	0	45	27	14	14	0	0	0	0	0	10·4	38
1795	0	49	15	11	14	0	0	0	11	0	8·6	68
1796	9	47	18	18	8	0	0	0	0	0	10·8	53
1797	5	41	5	49	0	0	0	0	0	0	9·6	76
1798	2	51	0	47	0	0	0	0	0	0	7·6	73
1799	2	35	16	47	0	0	0	0	0	0	9·5	74
1800	3	58	11	26	0	0	0	0	2	0	9·5	76
1801	3	44	9	35	9	0	0	0	0	0	9·8	54
1802	2	49	6	22	8	0	13	0	0	0	10·8	37
1803	14	45	14	2	21	0	4	0	0	0	10·9	11
1804	6	66	13	2	5	0	8	0	0	0	14·4	4
1805	3	31	32	27	0	0	7	0	0	0	15·0	51
1806	2	40	20	14	0	0	14	6	0	4	14·5	31
1807	2	13	24	7	0	0	21	33	0	0	13·3	41
1808	6	14	14	35	0	9	12	3	1	6	14·5	64

Year												
1809	2	17	18	51	0	0	12	0	0	0	17·7	71
1810	3	24	5	43	10	10	4	1	0	0	19·3	63
1811	9	8	1	63	9	2	5	3	0	0	17·2	60
1812	18	8	4	29	8	9	11	13	0	0	17·5	25
1813	9	13	13	22	12	7	13	11	0	0	14·3	26
1814	5	5	16	25	26	9	8	7	0	0	11·2	32
1815	14	12	10	14	22	17	11	0	0	0	9·3	15
1816	20	30	35	0	7	0	8	0	0	0	9·3	0
1817	27	11	23	0	8	24	7	0	0	0	12·0	0
1818	21	13	31	0	9	26	0	0	0	0	11·7	3
1819	37	13	11	5	3	28	8	0	0	9	10·1	12
1820	26	21	14	7	0	26	0	0	0	5	8·8	11
1821	28	14	14	5	0	31	0	0	0	0	8·1	17
1822	28	13	10	0	0	44	0	0	0	0	7·0	7
1823	19	9	33	0	0	39	0	0	0	0	6·8	0
1824	21	11	21	0	0	47	0	0	0	0	3·2	0
1825	8	19	73	0	0	0	0	0	0	0	2·2	0
1826	41	21	17	0	0	21	0	0	0	0	2·0	0
1827	21	25	54	0	0	0	0	0	0	0	2·0	0
1828	33	25	17	0	0	25	0	0	0	0	2·0	0
1829	25	8	67	0	0	0	0	0	0	0	2·0	0
1830	18	18	64	0	0	0	0	0	0	0	1·4	0

short sea routes to France, the North Sea and the Baltic being offset by new opportunities in the longer haul Atlantic trades, especially the importation of timber from North America. Above all else, Henley's took advantage of the huge expansion of the transport service, in some years hiring more than half of their fleet to the government. In essence, the French Wars provided them with the opportunity to concentrate upon shipowning at the expense of their general merchanting business and this is reflected in the careful manner in which they built up their fleet and their willingness to send their vessels to many parts of the world.

References

1. For example, Parliamentary Papers (P.P.) 1806, XII and Public Record Office (P.R.O.) Customs 17/1–30, 36/5 for entrances and clearances of shipping at British ports.
2. See P.R.O., Board of Trade 107, 108.
3. R. Davis, *The Rise of the English Shipping Industry in the Seventeenth and Eighteenth Centuries*, London, 1962, p. 62.
4. J. A. Goldenberg, 'An analysis of shipbuilding sites in Lloyd's Register of 1776', *Mariner's Mirror*, LIX, 1973, p. 419.
5. Henley's also owned the *Maria* for periods between 1785 and 1791 which was built at Whitby. S. Jones, 'A maritime history of the port of Whitby, 1700–1914', unpublished Ph.D. thesis, University of London, 1982, p. 27 suggests that many Whitby built vessels were sold to London owners, especially after 1793.
6. 38 Geo. III, c. 76, stipulated heavy penalties for breaking convoy.
7. HNL/56/12.
8. P.R.O., Admiralty (ADM) 106/1532. Promiscuous In-Letters to the Navy Board, 1802–5, 'H'.
9. HNL/91/11.
10. HNL/48/9.
11. HNL/26/3. February, 1811.
12. HNL/15/9.
13. HNL/64/3. September, 1800.
14. HNL/119/4.
15. Davis, *English Shipping Industry*, pp. 77–8, believed most vessels over 200 tons were three-masted. Though Basil Lubbock, 'Ships of the period and developments in rig', in C. N. Parkinson (ed.), *Trade Winds*, London, 1948, p. 95 saw little difference between vessels with different categories of rig.

16. See J. R. Harris, 'Copper and shipping in the eighteenth century', *Economic History Review*, 2nd ser., XIX, 1966–7, pp. 550–68.

17. HNL/67/4.

18. HNL/114/10,17.

19. HNL/105/6.

20. HNL/43/1.

21. R. G. Albion, *Forests and Seapower*, Cambridge, Mass., 1926, pp. 76–7.

22. P.R.O., ADM 106/3522. Sale of naval ships, 1814–18.

23. The tonnage of ten out of a hundred of these vessels is unknown.

24. HNL/85/3. C. French, 'The trade and shipping of the port of London, 1700–76', unpublished Ph.D. thesis, University of Exeter, 1980, p. 208 suggests that increases in vessel sizes occurred in wartime when merchants chose to ship their cargoes in large, well protected vessels. However, by the time of the French Wars convoys were well armed and therefore individual protection was less important.

25. HNL/17/3.

26. HNL/15/10.

27. *Select Committee on East India built shipping*, 1813–14, p. 56.

28. HNL/15/11.

29. HNL/19/12.

30. HNL/19/11.

31. HNL/103/15.

32. Davis, *English Shipping Industry*, p. 376.

33. *Ibid.*, p. 376.

34. HNL/15/3.

35. *East India Shipping*, p. 142.

36. *Select Committee on Manufactures, Commerce and Shipping*, 1833, p. 213.

37. Newer vessels were more frequently found in those trades where the cargoes were more valuable and susceptible to damage. The financial penalties of ruining such a cargo were sufficient to bankrupt most owners. Newer ships may also have involved a greater degree of shared ownership so that a man of a similar financial standing to Henley could be involved in the operation of a fleet.

38. HNL/15/1.

39. *East India Shipping*, p. 115.

40. R. Craig, 'Capital formation in shipping', in J. P. Higgins & S. Pollard (eds.), *Aspects of Capital Investment in Great Britain, 1750–1850*, London, 1971, p. 141, suggests eight to twelve pounds per ton; Davis, *English Shipping Industry*, p. 375 estimates seven pounds to

nine guineas; C. H. Feinstein, 'Capital formation in Great Britain', in P. Mathias & M. Postan (eds.), *Cambridge Economic History of Europe*, London, 1978, VII, part one, p. 65, suggests £20 per ton for 1801–20.

41. *Select Committee on the Coal Trade*, 1800, p. 48.
42. HNL/59/1.
43. HNL/34/1 and HNL/105/1.
44. HNL/17/3.
45. HNL/15/20, HNL/16/3.
46. HNL/20/14, HNL/19/4.
47. *Select Committee on Foreign Trade*, 1820, p. 42.
48. *East India Shipping*, p. 146.
49. HNL/19/12.
50. HNL/123/18.
51. HNL/88/1. Captain Armstrong to Henley's, May 1816.
52. HNL/73/22, HNL/118/17.
53. HNL/25/20.
54. HNL/44/1.
55. HNL/119/33, HNL/127, HNL/82/96, HNL/114/35.
56. A. D. Gayer, W. W. Rostow & A. J. Schwartz, *Growth and Fluctuation of the British Economy, 1790–1850*, Oxford, 1953, pp. 217, 695, 709.
57. Albion, *Forests*, p. 337.
58. *Ibid.*, p. 338.
59. HNL/20/12.
60. C. Wright & C. Fayle, *A History of Lloyd's*, London, 1928, p. 183. *P.P.*, 1812–13, IX, 449.
61. Wright & Fayle, *Lloyd's*, p. 187.
62. HNL/48/32.
63. HNL/15/33.
64. HNL/15/15.
65. HNL/31/1.
66. HNL/77/5,22,38, HNL/15/22.
67. HNL/15/22.
68. HNL/15/22.
69. HNL/15/15.
70. HNL/15/20.
71. HNL/15/1. March, 1799.
72. Davis, *English Shipping Industry*, pp. 194–5 believed that most vessels operated continuously in the same trade in the eighteenth century but adds that war changed this routine. For a more detailed analysis of Henley deployment see S. Ville, 'The deployment of English merchant shipping, 1770–1830: the example of Michael and

Joseph Henley', *Journal of Transport History*, 3rd ser., V, 1984, pp. 16–33.

73. For the full deployment of *Freedom* see S. Ville, 'Wages prices and profitability in the shipping industry during the French wars', *Journal of Transport History*, 3rd ser., II, 1981, pp. 39–52.

74. L. Horsfall, 'The West Indian trade' in Parkinson (ed.), *Trade winds*, p. 180 suggested vessels in this trade varied from 200 to 500 tons and were not built specifically for the purpose.

75. For example, see *The Shipowner's Manual and Sea-Faring Man's Assistant*, Newcastle, 1804 and G. Harrison, *The Freighter's Guide and Corn Merchant's Assistant*, Newcastle, 1834.

76. The main coasting series begins in 1835.

77. HNL/107/14. Ireland was not officially classed as coasting until 1823 but is included here for purposes of simplicity and to avoid creating another geographical area.

78. See S. Ville, 'The size and profitability of English collier vessels in the eighteenth century: a reappraisal', *Business History Review*, LVIII, 1984, pp. 103–25 for a more detailed analysis of Henley deployment in the coal trade.

79. *Eighth Report of the Commissioners of Naval Enquiry. His Majesty's Victualling Department at Plymouth*, 1803–4.

80. HNL/101/3.

81. HNL/15/43.

82. See J. Potter, 'The British timber duties', *Economica*, new ser., XXII, 1955, pp. 122–36.

83. The timber magnates believed the ending of the French wars would cause a reversion back to the Baltic. Albion, *Forests*, p. 355.

84. HNL/77/22.

85. HNL/119/33.

86. HNL/42/5.

87. R. G. Albion, 'British shipping and Latin America, 1806–1914', *Journal of Economic History*, XI, 1951, pp. 361–74.

88. National figures for the period are incomplete and deal with entrances and clearances at British ports, thereby creating a problem of double-counting. See P.R.O., Customs 17/1–30, 36/5.

89. G. Jackson, *British Whaling Trade*, London, 1978, p. 61.

4 · The role of the master

The shipmaster's contribution to the success of a venture was of critical importance. His responsibilities form an exception to the normal concentration of ownership and control, with the early development of a form of salaried managerial class, albeit heterogeneous. By the later decades of the eighteenth century the supercargo[1] was rarely used. The agency system was developing[2] but its efficacy varied according to the trade and the influence of the particular shipowner and was limited to when the vessel was in port. Bad communications further weakened the agent's role and the owner's control. Therefore, many ventures were left in the hands of the master for months while the owner awaited news. Naturally, he constructed safeguards to ensure the safety of his vessel and the loyalty of her master; these included good wages and conditions, a proportion of the freight, along with some guarantee of future employment.

The choice of the captain has been seen as one of the three major decisions affecting the success of a venture.[3] His duties covered a very wide range of responsibilities of a navigational, commercial, legal, financial and personal nature. Besides appointing and handling the crew, he was responsible for the navigation of the ship, he supervised the loading and discharging of cargoes and signed the bills of lading, he dealt with agents and merchants which could often involve arranging new charters and haggling over freights; ship repairs, victualling and voyage accounts were also within his prerogative. In wartime, his duties expanded. He had to fit and maintain guns, ensure the safe storage of gun-powder and organise the defence of the ship if attacked; he had to safeguard the crew from the press gang, ensure the vessel sailed safely in convoy without too much loss of time, and grapple with the commercial problems of rapidly changing markets which characterised the war years.

A widening range of skills was demanded of masters in the eighteenth century,[4] especially with regard to literacy and navigational knowledge. By the end of the century all masters had to be literate. Letters between master and owner were an important source of commercial information and indicated how much longer the voyage would take, thereby enabling the owner to make future arrangements. Letters from the owner to the master acted as a means of advice and guidance. Masters would also have to be familiar with the growing number of mercantile and shipping guides.[5]

It is unclear how much formal education was required of masters; no indication is given in the Henley papers. The number of marine institutions was expanding to cope with the increased demand for masters engendered by the trade expansion of the industrial revolution and the French Wars.[6] The degree of literacy was important. Spelling was often a problem, with many masters writing phonetically. Confusing syntax presented difficulties of interpretation, causing Henley's to complain of ambiguity. It posed the most serious problems in the long haul trades where communications took longer and the issues discussed were less familiar. Moreover, since 'dog-leg' navigation was possible around the coast, the more literate masters were employed in the foreign trades. The degree of literacy improved with practice enabling masters like James Kirton to graduate from the home to the more lucrative overseas trades.

Numeracy was another requirement given the need to keep voyage accounts, sign bills of lading and draw bills of exchange, together with the demands of navigation. Here again a wide range of competence was displayed by different masters. All accounts were rigorously checked by Henley's and alterations in red ink were necessary with the worst kept accounts. For example, between February and May 1788, Henley's corresponded with Captain Ross concerning seven separate items in his accounts with the *General Elliot* during the previous year.[7] In 1821, when the Transport Board considered the appointment of clerks on board all transports, Captain Haden remarked:

It appears to me that such a person will be a great acquisition for we masters of ships are but poor book keepers & I firmly believe that the ignorance of many on that head is the means of owners losing a great deal.[8]

Checking of accounts was designed largely to increase efficiency. Embezzlement was indeed very rare and dismissals were generally for incompetence. Although masters had some latitude in the expenditures of the ship, a large and experienced firm like Henley's had a fairly precise idea of what the level of real expenditure should be for a given voyage. On the other hand, the volatility of prices during the French Wars made the task more difficult. Accusations against Captain Errington of the *William* in October 1817, in an anonymous letter, were unusual:

... a soon as the ship comes to Shields the masters wife goes abord and strips the cabbin of every thing as Tea, Sugar and candles and every other article that is required in a house last voyge the boys was carreing baskets of porter on shore to the masters on the Sunday morning so as [not] to atract public notice every voyge the best pieces of beef all goes from the butchers to the masters house and in short he entierly keeps his Family out of the ship.[9]

It is unclear how seriously Henley's took such letters and they continued to employ Errington for another year until the *William* was sold. The scope for 'fiddling' by the master was much greater when he was the only active owner.[10]

Personal attributes were also important since a master of doubtful character could prove disastrous. Owners kept well away from men who had any inclination towards drunkeness. In August 1810 James Kirton wrote of Robert Ions, who had captained several Henley vessels, that he had seen him drunk just once, 'people that loves Liquar is not to be depended on'.[11] Captain Latta, master of one of Kirton's own vessels, had to be confined to a lunatic asylum in December 1807.[12] Insanity from contracting venereal diseases was an occupational hazard and is illustrated in the gradual mental decline of Robert Pearson who had previously captained five Henley vessels:

He wander about power [poor] man take's little notice of anyone If he's asked how he is always answers he is better hopes to be imployed again by Mr Henley.[13]

Henley's stopped employing him before his decline became serious but in January 1815, the unlucky Kirton discovered that Captain Turner of his vessel *Snake* had also gone insane, making it impossible to fulfil a charterparty. The merchant generously agreed to cancel the charter rather than sue Kirton for his losses.[14] Following this, Joseph Henley wrote to Kirton warning him of the costly damages which could result. He gave the example of a local owner, Ward, whose vessel *Queen* had damaged a cargo of cotton. The merchant successfully sued for £25,000 damages,[15] a figure significantly greater than the value of the Henley fleet of the time. From the shipowner's point of view, Henley's had around £9,000 invested in vessel and freight for their ships returning from the West Indies during the French Wars. This far exceeded the amount invested in many of Arkwright's cotton mills.[16] All this gives a clear idea of the huge financial responsibility vested in the master; one bad captain could ruin a whole enterprise the size of Henley's. It may also help to explain why Henley's began in the bulk trades where cargoes were worth much less and graduated to the colonial trades when they could afford to withstand larger losses.

Since masters were a managerial class, possessed of particular qualities and an education, it comes as no surprise that they were from a higher social class than the common seaman. Although the increased demand for masters at the end of the eighteenth century may have enabled some to rise to this position from the lower classes. They were frequently the sons of minor merchants and others within maritime circles, so that, 'the boy going to sea with such a background could be sure that his early years were only a brief prelude to command of a ship'.[17] Richard Haden, master of Henley's *Star* between 1818 and 1821, illustrates this. His family owned a business in Wapping and were known to Henley's. One brother became a doctor and he himself was a keen reader of encyclopaedias and claimed his greatest enjoyment was music. In October 1809, Captain Pringle of the *Polly* was instructed to give particular training to the young Richard Haden so that he might soon become a mate;[18] and Haden in turn took his younger brother for accelerated promotion as an apprentice on the *Star*. For most men below the ranks of senior merchants, the captaincy of a good ship in a prosperous trade was a thing to be desired. Attainment of the position of master could in turn engender social promotion. It enabled Haden to make some money and move into the merchanting and shipowning classes. James Kirton, who was a Henley master and later a shipowner and merchant, considered himself a gentleman in the later years of his life.[19]

Privileges and the rise in status through shipping went hand in hand with great responsibilities and these were, probably more than in land-based management, constraints on simple, uncritical nepotism. A business of Henley's size had to pay attention to ability. Nor were the wide range of skills required of a master that easy to find. With the old-fashioned association of owners, held together by a managing owner, the master was often chosen as someone who could put money into the enterprise by buying a share. Alternatively, he might be the son of an owner. The owner/master relationship was very different for Henley's. Since they were sole owners of most of their vessels, they did not require financial inputs from outside, nor were they likely to yield to the social pressure of appointing the son of a friend. Thus they could end up with better captains by being able to pay more regard to personal qualities.

Patronage best describes the manner in which they appointed. Masters were frequently recommended for their abilities through intermediaries such as Kirton, Henley's agent at Shields. In June 1805, he noted of Andrew Carr: 'I believe him to be vary active sturing man, he's used every exertion to get the ship maned etc. I injoy that opinion of him, he will give a good account of himself, and give you every satisfaction.'[20] Kirton was proved correct. Carr went on to captain seven Henley ships in ten years and owned two vessels jointly with them. James Donkin became master of Lord Nelson in August 1816 as a result of a recommendation from Thomas Hurry, a Tyneside shipowner and repairer.[21]

Masters sometimes recommended men they considered suitable to take up a captaincy. For example, Robert Pearson suggested that Whyrill Park become master of the Norfolk,[22] on which he had previously been mate. This internal promotion was a regular feature of the Henley business. Frequently mates of one vessel were promoted to the captaincy of another by Henley's. Of about 129 masters employed by Henley's as many as thirty were promoted internally. Many of them were employed regularly over a number of years. As well as the Hadens, several other maritime families were a source of masters for example, the Pearsons, the Watsons, the Robsons and the Hillarys.

Masters did not often work their way up 'through the ranks'. They commonly went straight from apprentice to mate, and such was the demand for officers during this great period of expansion in the mercantile marine, that their average age tended to be surprisingly low considering their great responsibility. John Bowes, master of the Star between 1822 and 1824, was only thirty-four years old when he took up this appointment and since he had already been a master in the transport service for seven years and in the North American and Baltic trades for a further eight,[23] he was only about nineteen when he first took up a captaincy. Samuel Kelly, one of the few shipmasters whose memoirs survive, became captain of a vessel when only twenty-five years old as a result of coming from a maritime background.[24] Several Henley captains, such as Robert Blues, promoted their own sons to the position of mate as soon as they had completed their apprenticeship, though none passed on to the captaincy of a Henley vessel, probably reflecting the firm's suspicion of nepotism. In 1816 Joseph Henley had remarked, 'I have always found old men [as masters] in large old ships do best', again reflecting the emphasis they placed upon ability and experience.[25]

Most Henley masters came from the north east, especially Tyneside. Some came from Whitby and, further afield, from Essex, London, Liverpool and Scotland. Masters tended to have a specialised knowledge of trades connected with their place of origin. Henley's deep involvement in the coal trade explains why many came from the North-East. Many of their most capable captains came from here, rendering questionable the belief that Tyneside masters were rough and primitive in their methods.[26]

A distinguishing feature of Henley's was the way they engaged a 'pool' of regular masters who did most of the work and remained loyal to the firm for most of their working lives. Thirty-two masters were employed by them for five years or more and between them they completed three-quarters of the captaincy work of the firm. Their longest serving masters were David Smith who was employed for twenty-two years of voyages between 1804 and 1830, William Chapman for twenty-one and Robert Pearson for twenty. There were many advantages to regularly employing the same men. The firm became familiar with the general competence and special expertise of such masters and might rely upon their loyalty. Moreover, they would be familiar with Henley's policies: which agents and merchants were used in various ports and how they should react to particular situations. This was important since Henley's held strong beliefs in such areas as the recording of protests after even a small incident and the importance of not wasting time whilst in port.

For the masters the 'pool' held clear benefits. They were guaranteed regular employment, were offered the more prestigious and rewarding voyages and sometimes even a choice between several vessels. However, on one occasion, in April 1803, Stewart Omond, who had captained Henley vessels for seven years, complained: '... But when stringers Coms and geats good ships and handey ones and oald servents Bad ships and unhandey ones it apers that [if] I am not wirthey of a better ship then the *Ladey Julana* I think I am not wirthey of Eany.'[27] The *Lady Juliana* was twenty-five years old but within a month he had been transferred to the *Freedom* of only twelve years. Omond was too valuable to alienate. Henley's was a large and influential firm and for a master to have worked regularly for them over a number of years and to receive a good reference was clearly very useful. They paid regular masters retainers between commands especially when they were particularly keen to keep a master for a forthcoming voyage. The captain's wife was often employed as paymaster to the families of her husband's crew.

These captains built up a close relationship with Henley's which served them well in the long run. For example, the firm helped the families of such men out of distress on their death. Some were offered a share in a ship owned by Henley's, a good offer given Henley's expertise and success. Sometimes they were given alternative employment with the firm when they became too old for the sea. James Kirton became Henley's agent at Shields and Francis Watson acted as a clerk for them. Kirton had also supervised the construction of the *Freedom* at Stockton in 1791[28] and Robert Harwood travelled around various ports in 1799 looking for a shipbuilder willing to build Henley's a new vessel.[29]

In general Henley's did not keep masters employed on the same vessel for long periods. Robert Ions, master of the *Friendship* for eleven consecutive years, was exceptional. Masters normally switched vessels every few years or so. The more competent regular masters could be expected to handle any size of vessel up to about 400 or 500 tons. John Armstrong captained nine Henley vessels in only seven years and Robert Watson five in only six years. The ability to move a master from one vessel to another gave Henley's greater manoeuvrability in their operations, especially if the master and his ship were not simultaneously ready for fresh employment. The command of larger vessels in excess of about 300 tons was beyond the capabilities of some captains who were unlikely to be kept in the pool. In 1821–2 George Atkinson captained the *Star* for a transport voyage in the Mediterranean. A report on his competence stated: 'Capt Atkinson has settled his Accounts with me perfectly correct and satisfactorily and I believe him to be a good sailor and very capable of taking the charge of a small vessel, but I do not consider that he carries sufficient command amongst the crew of so large a vessel as the *Star*.'[30] Presumably the report believed Armstrong was incapable of maintaining discipline and standards of seamanship amongst a numerous crew. A larger ship, though, was also more demanding with respect to her handling, cargo trimming, freight arrangements and accounting responsibilities. This was the last time Atkinson commanded a Henley vessel. Although masters were moved from one ship to another, by remaining with the same vessel they would have become more familiar with her technical handling, such as manning and stowage requirements. Richard Haden of the *Star* demonstrated the attachment which a master could feel for a vessel:

I stood ashore to see my much loved wooden wife pass & I assure you that it was a circumstance of real pleasure & regret ... the first because she looked so well & every body spoke well of her, the latter because it seemed that I were losing a much attached friend, with whom I had for some time been on terms of the greatest intimacy.[31]

Henley's must have considered the economic advantages of moving masters around to be greater than the technical economies accruing from keeping the same masters and ships together. This was partly due to the fact that they may have regarded their business as one overall operation rather than viewing each ship as a separate enterprise. Thus the performance of the business as a whole was more important than that of individual vessels. Most Henley vessels were deployed flexibly; masters being somewhat more specialised were moved from one vessel to another according to their deployment.

The specialised knowledge of Captain Robert Gardner in the West Indies trade was crucial in obtaining reasonable freights in 1816–18 when there was a glut of ships sailing there. In nine years he took three Henley vessels to the West Indies. Gardner came from Liverpool which helps to explain his expertise in this trade.

Coasting was probably within the competence of all masters,[32] but the West Indies and South American trades presented greater difficulties. Navigation was more difficult owing to climatic problems and imperfect knowledge. Samuel Galilee, whose own vessels had been to the West Indies, supplied

Henley's with detailed written instructions regarding navigation in the Caribbean.[33] Commercial problems also existed in bargaining with the merchants for a freight, deciding how to load it and in what proportion to mix different produce. In March 1817, Captain Gardner obtained a freight for the *Star* by offering to take the goods at 6*d* below the current freight rate: 'The other ships that were standing out have now agreed to reduce the freight 6d, which if they had done before me, I would have been cut out, as they were in the island so long before me.'[34] West Indian produce, as well as being highly valuable, was also very susceptible to damage and thus the master had to ensure it was carefully and safely loaded. There were far fewer problems involved in the coastal and Baltic trades where the commodities were less vulnerable to fluctuations in price and quality.

Robert Ions and Francis Watson each commanded a single vessel, deployed only in the coasting and Baltic trades for over a decade. Contemporaries distinguished between the coasting and the foreign trade master. 'I do not think Captain Dann exerts himself as he ought to do, or else the ship might be clear', the Dublin agent wrote of the master of the *Polly* in 1787. 'He has I think too much the manners of a coasting master (a phrase the sense of which I am sure you well know) to have the command of such a ship.'[35] A few days later it was spelt out: 'an honest man but with very little understanding'.[36]

Clearly then, the duties of going foreign, in terms of navigation, commerce, cargo handling and personnel management set the foreign trade master apart from the limited competence of the coastal one. Henley's gained greater flexibility from keeping foreign trade masters in their 'pool' who could be moved 'up'. However, experienced and able masters were unlikely to be satisfied for long running old colliers around, especially when their skills were in demand in wartime. Thus, Henley's kept on a few men like Ions and Watson to do much of the coastal work. Some of Henley's original coastal collier masters, such as Kirton and Dodds, managed to make the transition to foreign trading, thereby solving some of the firm's recruitment problems when they began to diversify into more trades. However, they still needed to bring in some skilled masters from outside, such as Robert Gardner.

William Chapman spent most of his time as a Henley master

working ships in the transport service which demanded a great deal of masters who had to cope with the voluminous information dealing with transport rules, convoy signals and other instructions, together with the dictatorial and condescending attitude of officers of the transport service and Royal Navy. Dodds of the *Eagle* came into conflict with the transport agents at Texel in 1799 when he was ordered to berth in inadequate water. His protests fell on deaf, or stupid, ears, 'I then sayd', he wrote home:

if you will make water for the ship I will gett hur to the wharf he then put his hand to my brest and shouved me back and sayd be gon you scoundrell ... another officer of the Navey came and pulled off my hat and throu it on the ground and sayd you fellow ought to keep of your hat when you speak to an officer of the Navey.[37]

Such were the demands of the transport service that many captains shied away from it whenever possible. Captain Omond claimed he would rather be the mate of any ship than be master of a transport.[38]

Not all Henley masters specialised in particular trades. Andrew Carr captained vessels to the United States, South America, the West Indies, Canada, the Mediterranean, the Baltic and the coastal trade. The system of pilotage removed some of the worst dangers from a master engaging in an unknown trade. In addition, the prearrangement of wartime freights by Henley's meant the master need know comparatively little about the commodity trades.

Competition between masters for command of the more prestigious ventures was fierce and rivalries often bitter. Stewart Omond's objections to a new man getting one of the better ships has already been shown. In January 1804, when William Pearson replaced John Thompson as master of the brig *Union*, the former wrote:

... since our arivall at Shields Mr. Thompson according to his usuall method in a Publick House has attempted to degrade me and enlarge him self at the expence of my character by saying he was mutch superior to me in evrey abilitey. I genteley caled him to account for his behaviour on board the Union which he abused me verrey disagreeably.[39]

In September 1796, Captain Robson commenced a legal action against Captain Omond for defamation of character,[40] and in

March 1812, Captain Darley conflicted with Alex Gillis who had been shipkeeper on board the *Zephyr* while she was laid up and refused to let Darley take any stores from the ship without a specific order from Henley's. Darley reacted by trying to throw him overboard.[41] Unauthorised removal of stores was, of course, a criminal act, and it was just as well that Gillis objected. Henley's could be very hard on masters who were negligent with their property, even to the point of absurdity. After only six months as captain of the *Lady Juliana*, Captain English incurred Henley's dissatisfaction by losing an anchor at Margate.[42] English objected pointing out that the weather had been severe and many vessels had suffered worse damage. Joseph Henley was unmoved. 'Your conduct', he wrote: 'is such that unless you come and settle with me before 10 o clock to morrow I certainly shall put another master on board the *Lady Juliana* ... it now lies with yourself.'[43] English repudiated blame – and was never employed again. His independent spirit was exceptional. Most masters, fearing for their livelihood, were submissive. They might be valued managers but it paid to agree with the owners. In March 1801, Henley's criticised Captain Cummins for the amount he had spent. He replied:

... and if I have offended you by so doing, I did not think I would, but if you will please to accept the bill I will thank you very much and will observe not to draw any more without your advice ... should the *Freedom* go unto Blackwell Dock or any other way where I will not have to be imployed in her I will come upp to London then I can settle everything with you.[44]

Inadequate communications and the decline of the supercargo had already made the master's responsibilities considerable, but the wars of the eighteenth and early nineteenth centuries further increased his burden. The most obvious problem was to avoid capture by the enemy. If attacked, the master had to decide whether to run, fight or surrender. Several Henley vessels fought off privateers, but were more often overcome. On none of the ten occasions when a vessel was captured did Henley's blame the master; it was an inevitable hazard of wartime. Of the nine Henley masters whose vessels were captured, the only one not re-employed was Francis Watson, who spent about eight years languishing in a French prison following the capture of the

Henley in 1806. By the time he returned to England he was no longer capable of going to sea and instead was employed as a clerk for the firm.[45] Even William Pearson who lost two vessels in two years through capture was employed for at least another decade. However, in January 1809 the *Norfolk* was captured during a transport voyage. Captain Coates bargained with his captors to ransom the vessel for £1,000. They agreed and released the vessel and all its crew except James Tate, the mate, who was kept as collateral. The Transport Board refused to indemnify Henley's since it was illegal to ransom a vessel. Henley's refused to pay the ransom money and so Tate remained in prison until the end of the war.[46]

The type of cargoes carried during wartime could create problems for the master. In January 1800, the *Ann* embarked 243 English prisoners of war at Flushing as part of an exchange agreement. Before the vessel sailed, an order came to disembark again whereupon the prisoners of war wielded handspikes and tried to force the *Ann* to sail but were eventually overpowered.[47] In June 1815, Captain Carr of the *Mary Ann* had trouble returning American prisoners of war:

... never did I experience such relief from misery as when the prisoners disembark'd last night ... about 4 hours after our arrivle here they tore the Ensign from the Main Top fr mast hd & took it on shore swept the streets with it & then tore it in pieces & I unfortunately coming thro them at the time on my road from the Custom House they insisted I should take the pieces as nothing belonging to the Bloody English should contaminate Yanky Ground & made use of much abusive & scandelous Language.[48]

The choice and handling of the crew was a major part of the master's work. The onset of war frequently exacerbated relations between master and crew. Wage levels fluctuated rapidly, creating a continual source of disagreement. In addition, the master had to arrange Admiralty Protections from impressment and try and release men pressed from his vessel. These points will be discussed in more detail in the next chapter. Certainly a more relaxed relationship existed between master and crew than in the Royal Navy and occasions of major conflict were rare. If the master was dissatisfied with the crew he would discharge them, whilst a seaman might desert. A problem existed of how far the master was responsible for the actions of the crew. In November 1805, the *Daedalus* had been blown close to the coast and, as a result, a cable had to be cut and assistance taken from shore boats. Captain Pearson asked Henley's not to hold him responsible for the negligence of crew members who had fallen asleep during their watch.[49] Persistent crew problems would naturally reflect on the master's competence.

Masters were generally paid by the month in the foreign trades and by the voyage in coasting. On taking up the captaincy of a vessel he signed a contract with the owner. When Andrew Carr took command of the *Norfolk* in May 1805 he was '... to have £10 per month (in foreign trades) & in coal trade £5 pr month & £5 each voyage made' and £5 per month if the vessel was laid up.[50] Masters were frequently offered 'fringe benefits' such as a food and drink allowance. Lodgings were provided while the ship was discharging in the West India dock. Many fringe benefits or 'backhanders' may have gone unrecorded. The example quoted above doubtless represented a notable increase in Captain Errington's real income.

More substantial benefits came in the form of primage. This was a proportion of the freight paid by the merchant to the master, normally on voyages to Central and South America and the West Indies. Sometimes primage amounted to more than the master's wages. For example, John Brand received wages (at seven guineas per month) of £102 18s and primage of £180 15s 1d for taking *Anna* to Berbice in 1813–14.[51] Primage was, however, a volatile payment. The accounts of the *Freedom* show it as £23 on total freight earnings of £2,381 on her 1802 voyage to Honduras,[52] £46 on £1,168 to Antigua in 1803,[53] only £27 on £4,827 to Honduras in 1806[54] but £139 on earnings of £2,899 to Surinam in 1807.[55] For the 1802 and 1806 voyages, primage was only 1% and then ½%, respectively, of total freight earnings. This tiny proportion was due to the fact that with the carriage of mahogany primage was paid as a fixed amount per log. When freight rates rose in wartime the real incidence of primage fell. Primage paid on voyages to the West Indies was normally a percentage of the freight and, therefore, increased with the freight rate during the wars. This was also the case when valuable goods like coffee, sugar, rum and cocoa were brought from South America. Thus on *Freedom's* 1807 voyage from Surinam primage was as much as 4½ % of freight earnings. The reasons why and when primage was paid are not entirely clear, though it was probably an extra reward for the additional problems and responsibilities of carrying cargoes like coffee and sugar.[56] Henley masters never received primage in the coal trade. From 1816 the term 'primage' was used interchangeably with '5% in lieu of port charges and pilotage'. The master may have taken the balance of this 5% once port charges and pilotage had been paid. Masters were credited with primage in full in their accounts with Henley's though there may have been deductions in agreement with the merchant. A further indication is given in a note written by Joseph Henley in 1804 referring to a voyage made by Captain William Chapman to Jamaica in *Hermes*: 'Primage on freight out JH [Joseph Henley] has not plased to Chapmans Cr if he collected the freight he would be Intitled to it not otherwise'.[57] Alternatively, on an Atlantic voyage, a master might be allowed to carry some goods on his own account freight free or charge freight to carry somebody else's goods. In voyages made to St. Vincent by *Freedom* in 1811, 1812, 1813 and 1814, this 'cabin freight' was £101,[58] £97,[59] £93,[60] and £43.[61]

The master's pay was not as responsive to short-term wartime fluctuations as that of the crew. Aside from cyclical fluctuations his wages were influenced by various factors, especially the type of voyage and his experience. War did exert a gradual upward pressure on his wages but without the same volatility and magnitude which characterised seamen's wages. Experienced masters like Kirton and Dodds were being paid £7 per voyage in the coal trade in the 1780s, whilst a less experienced master was receiving about £6 or even five guineas in the case of John Atkinson. From the outbreak of war in 1793, masters' wages began to rise with £7 to £9 being the average and, occasionally, even £10 being paid either for a coal voyage or per month in the foreign trades. During the first thirty years of the nineteenth century the normal rate of pay for Henley masters was £9 or £10 with no indication of a fall in the post-war years.

Money wages rose in response to high wartime prices, but real wages remained relatively stable. Unlike seamen, the supply of masters was not greatly affected by the war. They were not impressed into the naval service and there was always a large supply of mates eager for advancement, though rapid wartime promotion may have reduced standards of competence. Henley's were not afflicted with this problem because they were in a position to choose the better masters. The termination of the French Wars caused unemployment amongst masters as well as seamen. The attitude of the owner was of vital importance to the master's wellbeing. A long serving master who had performed well over a number of years might be supported by his owner who would pay him half wages during the long periods of the year when the vessel was laid up. In 1833 John Nickols suggested that owners were often reluctant to sell vessels during a depression since this would mean turning masters out of employment.[62] If the master held a share in the vessel he might be able to prevail on the owners to hold on to their capital and wait for better times rather than sell on a deflated market. Although Henley's often helped masters who fell on bad times after 1815, they would not let sentiments influence the sale of a vessel and towards the end of the war began to run down their fleet. Nor did they retain vessels during the depressed 'twenties' simply for the sake of masters. Indeed, they sold a number of vessels when the opportunity of a temporary upturn offered itself in 1824. When the *Star* was sold in 1824 it was particularly unfortunate for her master, John Bowes: '... I feel myself disappointed in losing employment and more so that the season is so far advanced that all vacancies are now full.'[63] Underemployment was a problem for masters though less so than seamen. The fortunate master would go on a long haul to, say, the West Indies and return some nine months later having earned a good deal of money including fringe benefits and was glad of a rest with his family. During this break from work he might be paid half wages by his owner. This stood in contrast to the inferior master who might get one or two voyages as master of a collier before being put out of work for a period.

Masters' wages varied little between ports.[64] Frequently, Henley's hired masters who lived in the north-east. Sometimes they would make their way down to London to sign an agreement with Henley's to command a vessel in the foreign trades. For coasting work they would take command of the vessel when she came up to the Tyne. In his accounts, a master may have entered his pay for a voyage from London to Shields and back to London.

On other occasions he recorded it as Shields to London and back again at the same rate.

The voyage and the type and size of the vessel had a slight influence on the master's wages. As master of the *Henley* between 1786 and 1789 James Kirton received £6 per month or per coal voyage. She was an old vessel of 181 tons. He then took charge of the *Holderness* until 1791 at £8, a larger vessel of 319 tons and only five years old. At the end of 1792 Kirton took command of the *Freedom* of 318 tons, just newly built for Henley's the pride of their fleet; his pay rose to £10. The importance of the vessel and Kirton's growing experience were the main factors behind these increases. There may have been some difference in pay between trades but this was only slight and difficult to distinguish from other variables. The master was paid a prearranged rate in his contract, according to competence, leaving the owner to decide on the trade according to his experience and the demand for shipping. Hence, in 1789–90, Kirton was receiving £8 to command vessels in the Baltic and coal trades whilst John Atkinson was only getting five guineas or £6 for the same work.

The owner's generosity also had a bearing on wages. In all respects of their business Henley's drove hard bargains and this is reflected in the remarks of Captain Darley: '... there is not any Imploy out of London but the Marster have more wages per month and more priviliage than I have add since I have been in it ... I have been a great slave to your ships ever since I have been in the Imploy'[65] (although Darley was defending himself against accusations that he was paying seamen too high wages).

In wartime the master's wages occasionally fell below that of his seamen as well as the mate and carpenter especially in coasting where primage or cabin freight were rare. Even on a long voyage seamen could make more money by deserting and then taking advantage of the shortage of seamen to demand a very high wage for the return passage on another vessel. However, the master's conditions of employment were far superior and his position on board ship far more desirable. He knew that his wages were only temporarily less and he had the guarantee of relative stability in his income. He was also likely to benefit from a range of fringe benefits and unrecorded backhanders. The master benefitted from the French Wars in a number of ways, particularly by more regular employment, higher wages and quick promotion, but his conditions became more precarious. The threat of capture and imprisonment in a French or Spanish prison was a haunting fear. This fate was endured by nine Henley masters. Most of them managed to escape or be released within a year or two but James Mather and Francis Watson were severely affected by this experience. Watson was kept in prison for about eight years and on his return to England never went to sea again. His desperation was reflected in a letter in May 1808, a year and a half after being captured: '... please God I return to my native Country agane it is hard living hear everything verry dear on account so many prisoners.'[66] Mather was imprisoned in 1808 and remained there until 1814. When he returned he found that his wife had run up large debts. Henley's refused to employ him because he would disrupt their plans if he was taken away for debt.[67] Several years later they rescinded and took him back again.

As well as sharing some of the managerial responsibilities of a large shipping business, the master could help to expand its capital. Henley's shared just eleven vessels with masters, four with Stewart Omond, three with William Dodds, two with Andrew Carr, one with John Ladd and one with Bartholomew James. James took the *Maria* to the West Indies and sold further shares in her to merchants from the Caribbean. Omond had captained Henley vessels for thirteen years, Dodds for twelve and Carr for four before they owned vessels with Henley's. For Henley's this helped achieve the optimum size for the efficient operation of their business. For the master it was an investment of which he had some knowledge and was a natural graduation into shipowning which might offer a guaranteed income once he was too old to go to sea. It also represented a further devolution of managerial power from the owner to the master. The share-owning master would take command of the vessel and be allowed more latitude in decision-making than usual. Though, clearly, his influence was still much less than if the other owners had been passive investors. A majority of these shared ships were owned between 1809 and 1812 when the firm was at its largest which suggests that the advantages for Henley's were both managerial and financial. The shared ships during these years were generally sent out tramping which sets them apart from the firm's normal wartime approach of pre-arranged charters. Only two of these shared ships were kept for more than three years because the prosperous war years were drawing to a close. The *Eagle*, owned with William Dodds between 1796 and 1802, when it was stranded off Yarmouth, was one of the firm's most successful vessels.

The idea that masters were encouraged to have a share in the vessel they captained so that they would perform efficiently and not abscond was not true of all cases.[68] Examples of abscondence were rare and this was no sensible proposition for sane captains. Maintenance of favour with the owner was a strong motive for efficient conduct. The fact that Henley's had long known the masters with whom they went into ownership shows that the need for loyalty and reliability were not the reasons. Instead, these men had proven abilities and would be considered worthy business partners. The combination of master and merchant, though not owner, in one person seems to be very rare. There is only one Henley example of this when John Brand was both master and freighter of the *Anna* for a voyage to Berbice in 1811–12.[69] Although masters did have commercial responsibilities in connection with goods carried on board ship, the natural progression was from master to owner rather than to merchant. This may be yet another facet of the growth of the specialist shipowner and the decline of the merchant shipowner. Nor was it common for the merchant who had hired the vessel to have a say in the appointment of the captain.

The decline of the supercargo, the embryonic nature of the agency system and the special demands of war combined to make the master's task cumbersome and his judgement critical. His remit stretched across a wide range of technical, commercial, financial and personal fields, reflecting an early, and possibly unique, example of the divorce of ownership from control. Masters normally came from merchant backgrounds because literacy and patronage were important prerequisites. However, ability rather than nepotism was recognised by Henley's as essential for the operation of their business. A distinction has been drawn between the highly competent master, capable of handling various vessels in many trades and retained over a long period by the firm, and the less able captain employed periodically in the coastal trade. The modern equivalent of the latter might be a foreman rather than an executive, being far less involved in the taking of important decisions. Wages was only one of the benefits of captaining a vessel, primage, cabin freight, allowances, good living conditions and a miscellany of backhanders must also be included. Some masters were even offered the opportunity of buying a share of one of the firm's vessels. From Henley's point of view it created the possibility of extending the capital of the business and devolving more responsibility, but for the master it presented the exciting and potentially lucrative opportunity of combining forces with one of the foremost shipowners of the day. Nonetheless, as in all their dealings, Henley's drove hard bargains with their masters and quite clearly achieved good returns on the money spent on employing captains. There are several indications, quoted above, that Henley's may have paid slightly less than other owners. This may be the case but the fact that they were able to retain the services of many highly competent masters over long periods of time suggests it could not have been all that bad.

References

1. A supercargo was a representative of the shipowner who travelled on board the ship and dealt with commercial matters in connection with the vessel and her cargo.
2. See R. B. Westerfield, *Middlemen in English Business*, New Haven, Conn., 1915, especially chs. 4 and 7.
3. R. Davis, *The Rise of the English Shipping Industry in the Seventeenth and Eighteenth Centuries*, London, 1962, p. 174.
4. Davis, *English Shipping Industry*, pp. 122–3.
5. See Robin Craig, 'Printed guides for master mariners as a source of productivity change in shipping, 1750–1914', *Journal of Transport History*, 3rd series, III, 1982, pp. 23–35.
6. For example, Trinity House School, Hull, was opened in 1787 to teach navigation. See G. Jackson, 'The foundation of Trinity House School, Kingston-upon-Hull: An experiment in marine education', *Durham Research Review*, 21, 1968.
7. HNL/63/15.
8. HNL/114/17.
9. HNL/124/3.
10. See A. F. Humble, 'An old Whitby collier', *Mariner's Mirror*, LXI, 1975, pp. 59–60.
11. HNL/15/11.
12. HNL/15/8.
13. HNL/15/27, Kirton to Henley's, July 1815.

14. HNL/15/27.
15. HNL/15/27.
16. S. D. Chapman, *The Early Factory Masters*, Newton Abbot, 1967, p. 128. The total capital invested in five of his mills varied from £1,500 to £4,000.
17. Davis, *English Shipping Industry*, p. 117.
18. HNL/108/14.
19. *Directory for Northumberland and Durham*, Newcastle, 1827, p. 285. Kirton is referred to as a gentleman of King Street, South Shields.
20. HNL/99/20.
21. HNL/82/47.
22. HNL/99/14.
23. HNL/114/29.
24. C. Garstin, *Samuel Kelly*, London, 1925, pp. 167–8.
25. HNL/19/11. Nothing is known of the age structure of Henley's pool of masters.
26. Jon Press has written, 'Geordie masters were often uncouth drunkards who ruled their ships with boot and fist', 'The Economic and Social Conditions of the Merchant Seamen of England, 1815–54', unpublished Ph.D. thesis, University of Bristol, 1978, p. 57.
27. HNL/77/38.
28. HNL/59/1.
29. HNL/17/3.
30. HNL/114/28.
31. HNL/114/24.
32. Though Captain Ross of the *General Elliot* had remarked about taking a captaincy in the coal trade, '... no man is equal to but those bread up in it from their youth'. HNL/63/15. It could be very dangerous; in bad weather conditions the loss rate was considerable, leading to the construction of harbours of refuge which were financed from taxes on the coal trade.
33. HNL/59/76.
34. HNL/114/2.
35. HNL/107/14, Isaac Weld to Henley's, December 1787.
36. *Ibid.*
37. HNL/48/16.
38. HNL/99/27, September 1808.
39. HNL/120/4.
40. HNL/34/15.
41. HNL/126/2.
42. HNL/77/16, February 1795.

43. *Ibid.*
44. HNL/59/55.
45. HNL/70/105, 120.
46. HNL/99/40.
47. HNL/34/28.
48. HNL/88/1.
49. HNL/45/8.
50. HNL/99/23.
51. HNL/37/9.
52. HNL/59/58.
53. HNL/59/61.
54. HNL/59/72.
55. HNL/59/76.
56. Davis, *English Shipping Industry*, p. 146 suggests that primage was paid by the merchant to the master and seamen as a gratuiuty for loading and discharging the cargo. There is no clear indication that seamen on Henley vessels were paid a proportion of the primage, even if they loaded or discharged the cargo.
57. HNL/72/1.
58. HNL/59/90.
59. HNL/59/92.
60. HNL/59/95.
61. HNL/59/98.
62. *Select Committee on Manufactures, Commerce and Shipping*, 1833, p. 349.
63. HNL/114/35.
64. Davis, *English Shipping Industry*, p. 135, believed masters' wages were higher in London than the outports in the eighteenth century.
65. HNL/77/65, May 1814.
66. HNL/70/105.
67. HNL/37/4.
68. Davis, *English Shipping Industry*, p. 127.
69. HNL/37/2.

5 · The pay and conditions of the crew

Henley's built up an important and successful fleet during the French wars. But it was also a period of serious disruption in the supply of seamen. The Royal Navy had no regular seamen before 1830, but raided the mercantile marine for wartime recruits. The result was retarded voyages, high wage costs and general uncertainty for shipowners. In such difficult circumstances, Henley's achievement takes on an even greater lustre. Moreover since we know little of the life of mercantile, as opposed to naval, seamen the Henley papers offer a valuable corrective to Dr. Johnson's assertion that a seaman's life was worse than a prisoner's, 'for being in a ship is being in jail with the chance of being drowned'.[1]

Many thousands of seamen served on Henley vessels and their experience offers an important insight into their background, pay and conditions. Pay, discipline, safety and length of service were all more favourable in the mercantile marine and to be pressed from here into the Royal Navy was one of the worst fates which could befall a seaman. The French Wars exerted a strong influence upon the lifestyle of seamen; the twin benefits of higher wages and more regular employment need to be set against the threats of impressment or capture by the enemy. This chapter will also look at apprentices, cooks, carpenters and mates and evaluate the significance of all these groups to the development and operation of the Henley business.

Most seamen came from the lower ranks of society and were recruited and often born in coastal towns and ports. Many of those who worked Henley vessels were recruited from Tyneside, although London and Portsmouth were also important places of hire.[2] Physical fitness was necessary and may have been reflected in a relatively low occupational age structure. The average age of nineteen seamen on board the Lady Juliana in July 1793 was twenty-three, the youngest being twenty and the oldest thirty. On the other hand, the mate was thirty-eight and the cook forty-five.[3] The age structure may have varied between trades. Conrad Dixon[4] believes seamen began in the coasting trade; as they matured they would be put into deep sea operations but would later return to coasting because of waning physical capacity. Jon Press[5] believes that young seamen were mainly in the foreign trades, transferring to short hauls and coasting as they grew older. Amongst Henley vessels, both young and old worked the long hauls, whilst the coasting trade frequently required greater physical exertion and was therefore composed of many young men. Personal factors complicated the issue: the unwillingness of seamen and their families to move, or a personal preference for, and greater experience in, one particular trade. In wartime, the high demand for seamen allowed them some choice between areas and trades. The cook may have been a former seaman, too old to perform full duties. In socio-economic terms, there was a distinction between able-bodied and ordinary seamen, characterised by higher wages and a completed apprenticeship. Wartime shortages of seamen led to the use of landsmen, foreigners and young lads (not always apprenticed), making it difficult to distinguish the typical seaman.

Insufficient evidence exists regarding literacy amongst seamen. They rarely needed to use the written word; some wrote home helped by a literate member of the crew or a notary but few such letters survive. On wage receipts they had to sign their names or, failing this, put a cross, though this might not constitute literacy since many simply learned to sign by imitating the shape. From a sample of 907 wage receipts of seamen from thirteen Henley vessels, 445 appeared to be literate, 370 illiterate, sixty-nine doubtful and twenty-three very doubtful. Therefore, at least 40% of these seamen were illiterate. These figures show a somewhat higher level of literacy than may have been expected and may suggest that some men, though lacking a formal education, gradually acquired at least a low degree of literacy through experience.[6] Nonetheless, many remained largely illiterate throughout their life which prevented promotion to mate or master.

There is little evidence to suggest that seamen were employed on a regular basis in Henley vessels. No roll or register of seamen was kept by them. Hiring of seamen was, instead, the responsibility of the individual master. Only occasionally were Henley's involved in the hiring of seamen, either as a favour for a friend or, if a master reported an acute shortage of seamen in an outport, they might send a few from London. Sometimes, this meant working through crimps whom Henley's generally paid two guineas per man hired.[7] Only on one occasion, in March 1822, was there an indication that several seamen had worked regularly for them.[8] In general, there was a very high rate of turnover of seamen, most being employed for only a few short hauls or one long haul. Death, desertion and impressment added to the casual nature of employment. When *Pitt* voyaged to Cuxhaven in 1805, a total of eighteen seamen were employed during the venture on a ship normally requiring only six or seven hands. Of these, nine deserted, one was pressed and one taken away for debt.[9]

Manning levels varied a good deal and depended upon the master's judgement, the capabilities of the men hired, the size and character of the ship, the trade, the availability of apprentices and the level of wages. Manning had fallen continuously over several centuries from around twelve men per hundred tons in the mid-seventeenth century, to six in the late eighteenth and four in the mid-nineteenth century.[10]

Wage receipts for Henley vessels broadly confirm the conventional wisdom. They also indicate the degree to which manning could vary in the short run. When seamen were lost during the course of a voyage for reasons of death, desertion or impressment, they were not always replaced by the same number. The master may have decided that the remainder of the crew were particularly capable or incompetent and take advantage of the turnover to change the manning level. In September 1803 six men were pressed from the *Hermes* but Captain Chapman hired only three replacements, leaving five men to do the work which eight had previously performed.[11] Chapman promised them extra money for this which he never paid. Masters frequently had problems finding a full complement at Portsmouth since it was both a naval base and the departure point for many convoys. In April 1805, Captain Grant of the *Valiant* bemoaned: '... if this men (crew) should get the better God knows whow I will get men for there is non to be had hear for love nor money'.[12]

Masters had different views on optimum manning levels because of their degree of willingness to take risks and the amount of work which they could obtain from the crew. The capabilities of a given crew varied according to their personal strength and skill. In April 1814 Captain Darley of the *Lady Juliana* wrote of the crew, '... so many small and light that we have the greatest difficulty to get our anchor'.[13] In June 1806 Captain Carr of the *Freedom* believed none of his crew to be worthy seamen.[14] The character of a vessel, her arrangement of sails and masts and the general condition of her stores could influence the number required to man her: 'I must be under the

Nessity of gating a man mor as sun as I can for we cannot gat the anker up and the rops are so thick and out of Propporshon that the *Freedom* I would sounr wirk with eleven hans then the *Norfolk* with thirteen.'[15] The *Norfolk* and *Freedom* were of the same size. In general, a larger crew was required on the longer hauls because of greater losses through disease and death. Coastal vessels were frequently rigged as brigs which, having only two masts, required less labour. Coasters were normally at sea only a few days, nor did the crew generally load and discharge coal cargoes. On short hauls second mates were unnecessary and carpenters frequently not used.

The experience of the 181 ton *Henley* between 1786 and 1806 provides an interesting example of manning levels. In the first few years two seamen along with a cook, carpenter, mate and master were employed in the Newcastle to London coal trade, although an extra hand was hired when she went to Portsmouth, Plymouth or the Baltic. In 1789 no carpenter was used when Francis Watson moved from this position to mate but three or four seamen were now hired in the London coal trade. In 1790 only two or three seamen were used, probably as a result of impressment and higher wages. The number of seamen rose again to four in 1791–2 before dropping back to two or three with the outbreak of war in 1793. Watson became master in 1794 and employed a carpenter but reduced the number of seamen by one. In 1797 the number of seamen rose to four once because of lower wages and promoting an apprentice to seaman. Between 1803 and 1806 impressment and high wages encouraged Watson to use only two or three seamen. Throughout this period, two or three apprentices were additionally employed on board the *Henley*.

The French Wars served to accelerate the decline in manning ratios.[16] Higher wages and a shortage of men acclimatised masters and men to using smaller crews. The abortive seamen's strike of 1815 had, as one of its chief objectives, a return to the higher prewar manning ratios of six men per hundred tons. The need to arm merchantmen in wartime had no appreciable effect on manning.[17] Most vessels carried few guns and did not hire specialist gunners. Crew members were instructed in the use of guns but engagements of the enemy were rare and shortlived.

Wartime manning reductions were also achieved by substituting cheaper apprentices or landsmen for able-bodied seamen.

The wartime suspension of the Navigation Laws, which had required four-fifths of the crew to be British, enabled Henley's to hire foreign seamen in significant numbers. In 1805, three out of six seamen on the *Pitt*, bound for Memel, were foreign[18] and three of seven when she sailed to Copenhagen two years later.[19] In 1796, four Frenchmen, probably prisoners, were employed on the *Concord* for no wages, although Henley's normally paid foreign seamen about the same as British.[20] However, foreigners never constituted more than about half of the crew and must have been considered less suitable than British seamen since Henley's complained to the Admiralty during a 'hot-press' that it was unsafe to proceed with an entirely foreign crew.[21]

In practice there were limitations on undermanning. A smaller crew increased the risk of losing the vessel in bad weather. Given the high wartime insurance rates, many owners did not insure their ships and therefore considered undermanning an unacceptable risk. If the ship was insured a claim might be invalidated if it was proved that the vessel was undermanned. Charterparties stipulated that the vessel had to be 'well and sufficiently manned'. Undermanning was most likely in the coal trade where vessels were old and cargoes generally carried on the shipowner's account, though it was still restricted by the reluctance of seamen to work on a vessel with obviously insufficient hands and the huge physical exertion required in the coal trade. Henley's appear successful in their manning policies, achieving cost economies without dire consequences for their vessels. Inefficient seamanship may have slowed down a vessel's movement though this is difficult to judge and may be more closely related to external factors, especially convoys.

The area of highest manning by far during the French Wars was the transport service where charterparties stipulated a ratio of five men and one boy per 100 tons measurement. This was about twice the number used in coasting. Owners and masters of transports tried to get away with using fewer than the stipulated number and crews were frequently mustered in an attempt to stop this practice. This led masters desperately to scrape around for extra men, if they had advance warning, or face being mulcted several days pay. There were several staggering examples of undermanning on Henley transports. In December 1805 the *Pitt* of 330 tons was mustered at Cuxhaven and found to be five men and one boy short.[22] Sometimes transports were temporarily undermanned because of losses through death and desertion. The agent still had little sympathy for the master, realising his willingness to underman purposefully, including the use of apprentices to imitate seamen during musters.

Discipline on board merchant vessels was not harsh compared with that on naval vessels. This is not to say that conditions were good,[23] or grievances unknown. Captain Owen of the *Mary* had difficulties with a seaman who was unwilling to come on deck during bad weather, could not steer properly, demanded his wages in an insolent manner and in only thirty days on board consumed £30 worth of provisions, '... the people declared to me that a 5 or 6 pound piece of beef was nothing in his way at a Meale'.[24] Captain Chapman of the *Lady Juliana* discharged seaman Featherstone for being in an almost permanent state of drunkeness[25] and Captain McClelland of the *Lord Rodney* had an aggressive argument with a seaman who wanted to go on shore rather than work on board,[26] though admittedly, imprecise conditions of employment, especially the number of working hours and precise duties, led to disagreements between captain and crew.

The problem became more serious if the master came into conflict with several seamen or the whole crew. Sometimes an individual spurred on others; James Smith was dismissed, '... on account of his bad behaviour holding the ship constantly in a state of mutiny'.[27] Drink was frequently the cause of unrest. In February 1813 nine of the crew of the *Polly* became very drunk, leading to a near riot during which one man fell overboard and drowned.[28] In August 1812, Captain Atkinson of the *Europa* suspected the crew of pilfering several puncheons of wine from the cargo.[29] Captain Dann of the *Polly* had particular difficulties with an Irish crew which caused him to write to Henley's:

But who can tell the deceit and wickedness of the Irish – they are even ashamed of themselves – for it proved I am beset with drunkards Heavy Headed fellows not worth a name. Even my mate – for at sea in bad weather or even fine I have much ado to see them on deck & in port I find to my sorrow they will be ashore ...[30]

Dann went on to remark that they 'stowed away' (ate) three and a half to four pounds of beef per day each and 'were so heavy as they could not find the deck'.[31] Henley's, it would appear, did

not under provision their vessels! Conflict arising from drunkenness, incompetence, greediness or even theft could be quelled
quite easily by discharging the crew or some similar measure.
However, in August 1792 Captain Edward Robson of the *Pitt*
faced a violent mutiny by a crew who refused to raise the anchor:

> I have gott the Completest sett of Blackguards on board that I ever sailed
> the seas with ... I sent for them into the Cabin and told them the Con-
> sequence of detaining the ship after sineing Arteals and that the owner's
> whould punish them – a fellow that I shiped at Gravesend told me that
> if all the merchants in London was shipowners they could not hurt
> him ... not knowing thease fellows intensions ... would not rigg the
> booms out where thay collected themselves to gather and Roberts con-
> tinued to give me very Instant Language I then told him if he whould
> not hold his tongue I would thresh him he still Continueing in this
> insetant manner and not going to his duity but told me he whould thresh
> me in London and thay keeping them selves to geather forward I ordered
> my mate to go forward with me and takeing a pistole in one hand and
> a piece of leadline in the other he still continueing in his Instant Language
> I gave him a few strocks with the line he then made answer that's all
> I wanted at the same time my boy Joseph Stevens heard Thos Sharpe say
> he whould give me a kink of the neck and one George Ayer said he
> whould nocked me down had not the mate been with me ... I have onley
> to say that my life is not safe with such fellows.[32]

However, greedy Irish, lazy or rebellious crews were the exception rather than the rule and most voyages passed without
incident.

Conflict was more enduring when it reflected deeply held
grievances regarding wages and conditions. Some historians have
claimed the existence of collective consciousness[33] among seamen emanating from economic rather than political
grievances.[34] Contemporary correspondence and reports of
unrest confirm that economic issues were at the forefront.[35] It
was in the Newcastle coal trade[36] that the greatest degree of
consciousness among seamen existed, the same seamen regularly
worked the trade and frequently lived as a community in the
north-east making them one of the most concentrated workforces
in Britain. The trade was particularly demanding because of its
strenuous nature which tended to isolate particular groups of
men. Seamen, a dominant section of the community in Shields
in the later eighteenth century, were more likely to form similar

interests through communication.[37] Seamen's strikes were among the first recorded industrial disputes and by the late eighteenth century occurred regularly as in 1775, 1777, 1785, 1790, 1792, 1796, 1815, 1819, 1822, 1824, 1825, 1831.[38] The principal grievances were manning, wages and impressment. Intermittent warfare disturbed the normal pattern of life for seamen, galvanising them into collective action.

In 1815, the reduced demand for shipping had forced seamen's wages down and had caused underemployment amongst them. The seamen of the north-east went on strike in September, demanding a minimum wage of five pounds for the return voyage to London and a reversion to prewar manning levels.[39] Kirton described them as 'troublesom and unreasonable'[40] and said they wanted a Committee representing the seamen to supervise the manning of vessels, 'which never can be the case'.[41] Captain Blues of the *Cornwall* complied with their manning and wages demands but was prevented from sailing until all the other ships agreed.[42] In October, the military and naval forces were called in and pressured the seamen to accept some limited concessions on pay.[43]

The withholding of monthly money, which was paid to the families of seamen, was a frequent resort of masters troubled by an unruly crew:

... stop the monthly money of John Seawood who have behaved exceedingly ill and forfeited all his claims upon this ship: I fear it will be hard upon his wife; but as his conduct is such as to make me expect he will always whilst with me, be very troublesom & perhaps may run away.[44]

Another tool of workplace discipline was the threat of impressment, though, given the shortage of seamen, this was rarely used in wartime.

Conflict was not always class orientated; disputes between seamen were frequent, though most went unrecorded. Sometimes there was tension between Tyneside and London seamen. The influx of foreign seamen during the wars may have encouraged racial conflict and might explain the stabbing of Manuel Joaquim by Antony Joseph, on board the *Lady Juliana* in June 1813.[45]

Impressment was one of the greatest fears of merchant seamen.[46] The personal protection from impressment was the 'most precious document any man living in a coastal area could possess'.[47] Between 1792 and 1800 there was a 20% growth in the number of seamen in the mercantile marine but a 750% rise in those of the Royal navy.[48] Given the low wages,[49] harsh discipline, long service and generally bad conditions,[50] a strong element of compulsion in recruitment for the Royal Navy was necessary.[51] The methods of the impress service were arbitrary and pedantic; Henry Blake was pressed because another seaman's name had been scratched out of the protection and his added below.[52] In March 1808 Matthew English was pressed because 'they sead he was three quarters of an Inch taller than he was down in the protition'.[53] Many other pretexts were used to press men such as the fact that a protection had only a few days before expiry. Sometimes all protections were ignored. Captain Harwood wrote from the Downs in September 1801: 'The Impress here exceeds all ever I met with the will not let any thing in the shape of a man pass.'[54] Recruitment was often by sudden spurts of activity, suggesting desperate short terms effects for merchant vessels.[55] In May 1803, all six seamen from the *Neptune* were impressed even though a valid ship's protection was presented.[56] Six seamen were pressed from the *Maria* at Jamaica in July 1790 and seven when she returned to the Channel in October.[57]

The personal intervention of the master could sometimes stop men being pressed or secure their release. A clever master would keep his seamen hidden away when the press gang was operating. Communication between masters and owners gave some indication of when and where they were working:

... the press broak out here this afternoon which thay have sarched the Dockyard and the ships hear bt seing them cuming got my people out of the ship I think of getting them to lodging on shore untill a protaction cum as the press gang frequent the Dockyard I shall indeavour to keep delivring but shall have to hire some men.[58]

The lengths to which Captain Dodds was prepared to go suggests the importance he attached to retaining his crew. To find a new crew meant wasted time and higher wages. Moreover, a master's ability to protect his crew would affect the ease with which he could hire seamen in the future and prevent his present crew deserting.

Many masters and owners regarded the impress service as an

unfair intrusion into the commercial operations of shipping. Sometimes it led to ugly incidents. In April 1794 Michael Henley wrote to the Admiralty complaining that the crew of the *Queen* had all been pressed while delivering coal for the Navy in the Thames.[59] The Admiralty replied:

... the master of the Queen had abused the officer who boarded her, in a most insolent manner, & had taken up a handspike threatning to knock the said officer down, which from every appearance he would have done had he not been prevented. The Lds of the Admiralty do not think fit to order the men who have been impressed to be discharged.[60]

Thus, vessels working for the government were not exempt from the press. Occasionally, conflict between master and seamen in the mercantile marine may have led to voluntary recruitment. In July 1789 six seamen left the *General Elliot* at Plymouth and joined the navy.[61] However, this was exceptional particularly in wartime; the overriding impression from the Henley collection is that most seamen were terrified of the press gang. The effects of impressment on the seaman's family could be drastic. Mary Reed wrote to Henley's in March 1795 asking them to try and secure the release of her husband, stressing that she had three children to look after and, 'I have to ly in soon of another'.[62]

The large amount of statistical material in the Henley Collection has enabled the construction of a series of wage tables and indexes covering a range of trades. Previous evidence was sketchy, contradictory and related largely to the coal trade.[63] From the detailed Henley evidence one can gain a clear year by year and even month by month view of wage trends in many trades. After a period of relative stability in the late 1780s, wages rose steeply following the outbreak of war in 1793. They continued to rise in the next few years, especially during the labour shortage of February and March 1795. Lower wages in 1796 and 1797 reflected the return of many vessels from the successful campaigns in the West Indies. Campaigns in Malta and Egypt at the end of the 1790s pushed up wages once more, only to be followed by a reversal during the temporary peace. Invasion scares and Pitt's positive military policy caused wages to rise in 1803, whilst another significant upturn in 1809–10 may have been due to the 'cold war' with America. With the return of peace, seamen's wages collapsed in response to the reduced demand for shipping and therefore seamen. Thereafter, except for the temporary boom in the mid-twenties, wages remained low, mirroring the depression in the industry. Real as well as money wages increased during the Wars, frequently by at least 100%.

Although the general trend is clear, precise movements varied between trades because competition in the labour market was not entirely perfect.[64] Seamen's real wages in the Mediterranean stood at their peak at an index number of 222 in 1794, whilst in the Baltic a peak of 170 was reached in the same year. In the Honduras mahogany trade a peak of 186 was attained in 1803. Even within the same trade wages varied; in November 1793 anything from six to nine guineas was paid for a coal voyage between Newcastle and London. Davis[65] believed there was little difference in wages over various trades in the eighteenth century, whilst Press,[66] looking at the period after 1815, contends that wages were slightly lower on the long hauls because of the guarantee of longer continuous employment. Conversely, it might be argued, many seamen were reluctant to spend long continuous periods at sea, especially if they had families. Wages were paid by the month in most trades but by the voyage in the coal trade. The rate per coal voyage was greater than per month in other trades, given that seamen were often on board colliers for less than a month, this suggests a higher rate of pay in this trade. On the other hand, unless they found another berth almost immediately, this advantage would be lost through underemployment. Wages to the West Indies, Central and South America moved in a similar fashion throughout this period, those to the Mediterranean and Canada may have been five or ten shillings higher, though the evidence is patchy, whilst wages in the Baltic were some ten or fifteen shillings higher again.

The wage rate might vary from port to port. It has been suggested that wages were lowest in London and highest on the Tyne, Wear and Humber where seamen received five or ten shillings more.[67] However, Henley's generally hired seamen for the voyage when the vessel was about to leave Newcastle rather than London because more time was spent waiting for coal on the Tyne than in delivering it at London and therefore the ship's victualling costs would be lower. Moreover, there may have been a larger pool of labour, skilled in the rigours of the coal trade, to be found on the Tyne than on the Thames. Sometimes seamen were hired for the passage from Newcastle or London rather than the whole round voyage. If one compares the wages paid by Henley's for the passage from Newcastle with that from London, in thirty years the mean wage was greater from the north and in only nine from London, with most of the discrepancy occurring after 1800.[68] This might be explained by a greater degree of class consciousness amongst the Tyneside workforce, enabling them to obtain slightly higher wages than in London where the workforce was more heterogeneous and less cohesive. The rapid industrialisation of the North-East in the nineteenth century may have made it into a high wage area. Alternatively, the passage north in ballast may simply have been considered easier than that south, coal-laden.

The size and characteristics of a vessel had little effect on the wage level, though a seaman would choose to work on a new, coppered vessel rather than an old leaky one. In a period of labour shortage a master of an old leaky vessel might offer a few more shillings to prevent seamen signing articles elsewhere. Comparing the *Henley* and the *Freedom* confirms the minimal effect of the vessel on the wage rate. *Henley* was a small vessel of 181 tons and was 18 years old when the Henley's bought her. The *Freedom*, on the other hand, was newly built for the Henley's and was 319 tons in measurement.

In some trades, wages varied according to the season. This was most striking in the coal trade where, 'after the 1st of October they always expect an advance of wages in the coal trade of at least £1 per voyage'.[69] The size of the seasonal fluctuation differed considerably from year to year. In the winters of 1796 and 1797, wages were far above those for the summers of 1795, 1796 and 1797. During the winter the demand for coal on the London market, as a form of heating, increased but fewer seamen were willing to go to sea since weather conditions made voyages longer and more hazardous. If the Tyne was frozen for several weeks prices would rise on the London markets. Very few loaded vessels would be able to sail and therefore wages would fall. Once the snow had melted many shipowners would employ vessels which had been laid up, in order to take advantage of high coal prices in London, which would push up wages.[70] Adverse winds on the Tyne would have the same effect. In January 1800, when wages in the coal trade were reaching peaks of ten and eleven guineas, weather conditions were very bad and the Tyne was frozen for part of the month. Seasonal fluctuations were less important in the Baltic trade since this area was virtually inaccessible in the winter. Voyages to the West Indies were begun in the winter in order to coincide arrival with the sugar harvest.

The possession of a protection affected the wage paid in wartime. A seaman who carried his own protection would expect a higher wage than if he was covered by the ship's general protection. In September 1795, Captain Dodds of the *Freedom* suggested that a personal protection normally entitled a seaman to an extra guinea.[71] In July 1804, Captain Pearson of the *Pitt* observed that, '... having men in the protection must make a difference of one man in our ship's companey'.[72] In other words, the equivalent of one man's wages would be saved in costs by having a ship's protection, although this was less safe from the press than a personal protection. In May 1803, Henley's wrote to the Admiralty saying that they could only supply coal to Plymouth Dockyard on reasonable terms if their seamen were guaranteed against impressment, 'otherwise we must have old men that protect themselves at 24 guineas each'.[73]

The level of wages was additionally affected by the industrial strength of masters and seamen as groups or by the ingenuity of individuals. In January 1802 James Kirton aptly noted:

... it is a pitty but all Owners & Masters would come to a Resolution for the people to sign Artickels when the seamen enters first on board, It is tow much the habbet, not to sign before a sea tide comes by that Rule gives the seamen the advantage of them, it is not in the power of a few ships to brick through these rules, I am much supprised that the trade in general dis not come to that Resolution & fix the wages so that ships might live.[74]

Such unified action did not occur; instead masters tended to act unilaterally. During the strike of November 1792, the seamen forced an increase of pay to four pounds per voyage in the coal trade. However, Captain Robson of the *Pitt* managed to get round this, '... my people sine'd articles for three guineas but have a note for four to satisfey the mob'.[75]

Another means of keeping down wages was to hire men by the run rather than the voyage in the hope that rates would have fallen by the time the vessel was ready to make her return

passage. Alternatively, the master of a collier might try and persuade his crew to accept payment by the month. This would
generally leave the seamen with less wages. In February 1805,
Captain Smith of the *Ann* tried to persuade his crew to accept
wages of five pounds per month rather than nine pounds for the
voyage.[76] It was unlikely that more than a month would elapse
between the vessel leaving Shields and arriving there again after
unloading at London. Another subterfuge was to agree no fixed
wage when the articles were signed, the seamen to receive the
same pay as on other vessels then sailing from port. Sometimes
this worked fairly, but often the master paid the lowest amount
recorded among the other vessels, leaving the seamen with no
legal claim against the owner. A master might go to neighbouring
ports in search of seamen willing to sail at a lower rate. In
February 1805, when Captain Smith was in conflict with the crew
of the *Ann* he searched all the nearby ports, though without
success.[77] Cheap substitute labour was sometimes hired.

Seamen extorted more money from captains by jumping ship
at a foreign port in order to receive a much higher wage for the
return passage: 'I believe there is not such another place in the
world as Quebec is at present for sailors Running ... ships that
sailed with the last convoy add to pay 28 & 30 Guineas for the
run.'[78] An Act of 1797[79] attempted to remedy this evil by im-
posing fines upon masters hiring deserters and laying down a
model wages agreement, though in practice it became difficult
to prevent desertion. Of course, seamen frequently went on strike
for higher wages. One of the conclusions of the 1800 *Coal Trade
Committee* was that seamen's combinations had forced wages
up to their unprecedentedly high level.[80] Some years later,
Robert Carter, a ship broker, believed the unions had kept wages
up when other prices were falling and thereby contributed to the
unprofitable nature of shipping.[81] However, in the long run, the
seamen's unions could only have a marginal effect on wage rates.
It was neither their strengths nor their weaknesses which caused
the large rise in wages at the beginning of the war nor the large
fall at the end. The 1815 strike failed because of the over supply
of men after the war.

Given the casual nature of their work, underemployment was
frequently a problem amongst seamen. The increased demand for
seamen during the French Wars meant that they enjoyed a greater

regularity of employment as well as higher wages and after 1815 seamen could find less work as well as receiving lower pay. In wartime, short hauls, such as the coal trade, had offered very high wages, but after 1815 the longer voyages became more appealing as a guarantee of employment for a longer period. Standards of living were also influenced by the number of dependants. On a long voyage, a sum of money was paid to seamen's wives each month by allotment. Therefore, at the end of the voyage his balance of wages would be less than that of an unmarried seaman. The unmarried seaman would also have no rent costs to bear while on board. Victuals were provided free to seamen and therefore made an important contribution to real income. The quantity and quality of this food varied a good deal. Seamen in Henley vessels seem to have been well provided, with plenty of meat in particular.

The mate was the middle rung in the ladder between seaman and master and was responsible for encouraging obedience and hard work amongst the crew. He also shared some of the master's responsibilities such as supervising the loading and discharge of the cargo. He was appointed by the master rather than the owner on most occasions[82] and often followed the same master from one ship to another. He was, in practice, a skilled assistant to the master and therefore reliability and loyalty were important qualities. It was this fact, along with a natural tendency towards nepotism, which led many masters to appoint their sons as mate on the ship as soon as they had completed their apprenticeship. There are many examples of this on Henley vessels. Promotion from seaman to second mate or even mate sometimes occurred. David Cresty was a seaman on the *Henley* from August 1793 until March 1794 when he became mate but then died in December. The progressive promotion from seaman to mate and then master within the firm does not appear to have occurred, although Richard Haden was temporarily a seaman and later captained a Henley vessel.

A reasonable degree of literacy and numeracy was required of mates to read and sign documents. In a sample of mates of Henley vessels, at least 81 out of 85 were literate. A letter to Henley's from William Allerdice of Dundee in January 1812 makes interesting reading:

I served as second mate on board your ship the *Silus* Capt Robson upwards of two years in the transport service and I would not have left the ship but for the want of education. I have been at school ever since ... I have studied the art of navigation and I hope will be found qualified to act as Chief Mate.[83]

While the second mate was barely above a seaman, promotion to chief mate was of greater importance.[84] On the other hand, Captain Grant of the *Concord* dismissed his mate in February 1796, claiming that he was too much of a gentleman![85] It also gives an idea of the extent of training required to become a mate or master. Doubtless, they were trained in numeracy, literacy and commercial problems as well as navigation. Other skills such as seamanship, cargo loading and personnel relations were probably learned through practical experience on board. A master, natural-ly, would give more attention to the training of his own son or that of a friend.

Mates achieved greater continuity of employment than seaman through less so than masters; there were about 130 masters in all employed by Henley's, compared with around 500 mates. On average, each mate was employed for about a year. The master had fewer discipline problems with mates than seamen; the remarks of Captain Pearson of the *Heart of Oak* in August 1793 were exceptional: '... my mate has not been upon deck since I left London but has continued in astate of intocksication till yesterday. Between the hours of 4 and 6 O Clock he went out of the cabin windows & was instantly out of sight so that wee never sead no more of him.'[86] In November 1795, Captain Chapman of the *Lady Juliana* had his mate impressed for bad conduct.[87] Demotion from mate back to seaman for bad conduct was rare.[88] Moreover, the mate could normally be relied upon to support the master during any serious conflict with the crew. Since he was appointed by the master then he needed to keep on good terms with him. In some respects the mate fits the term 'labour aristocracy' but there are methodological problems in using this phrase especially in this early period. Mates were infrequently impressed, although in periods of very hot presses they, and even masters, were at risk.

The mate would be paid a pound or guinea, or several, above the seaman's wage rate. This could lead to him receiving a rather anomalous amount such as £7 6s which represented a seaman's wage of six guineas plus a pound increment. Therefore, his real wage did not rise proportionately by as much as the seaman's in wartime, since the money differential rarely changed. In the 1780s, seamen were normally paid £2 10s for the return voyage between Newcastle and London and mates £3 15s. In the early months of 1800 seamen normally received 10 guineas and mates £11 10s or £11 15s. On occasions, the differential was wider which indicated the willingness of a master to pay a higher wage to an especially loyal and competent mate. The mate possessed a number of benefits over the seaman. His living and working conditions were better, he was often given work on board the vessel before and after a venture, he enjoyed longer, continuous employment and he was only one step, admittedly not always taken, from becoming master.

The ship's carpenter occupied a skilled job commanding a rate of pay similar to the mate's. He generally possessed a similar degree of literacy and numeracy. The carpenter was required on land, especially for shipbuilding and other areas of the construction industry, therefore his employment on ship was affected by external demand factors. This could lead to an acute shortage of carpenters. If there was sufficient work ashore, or in the short hauls, he would be reluctant to go on long voyages which might also be alien to his normal employment conditions. This lead Captain Darley to write in December 1810 that the carpenters at Shields, 'will not go foregen on acct of the wages being so high a shore'.[89] However, their wages did not rise above those of the mate during the war years, possibly because this would have been unacceptable to the latter. Their shortage was mitigated by relinquishing carpenters on the short hauls or combining the posts of mate and carpenter, as with Francis Watson of the *Henley*.

Watson was the only carpenter who became master of a Henley vessel but was always kept in old ships, carrying inexpensive goods over short distances. Carpenters were only impressed during acute shortages. In August 1799 some press officers boarded the *Henley* saying they had instructions to impress carpenters from all homeward bound vessels. When they found that the carpenter was unfit to be pressed, they took a seaman instead.[90]

The ship's cook was normally the eldest or least skilled sea-man[91] and was paid about 5s more than the others. Alternatively, an apprentice would do the cooking and receive 5s in return. The simple meals generally eaten on board suggest that little skill was required of a cook. Complaints normally centred on the quality of the food itself rather than the mode of its preparation.

Apprentices were of great value to wartime shipowners as cheap substitute labour during periods of high wages and labour shortages. This is most clearly evinced when Captain Pearson, on binding two apprentices in May 1794, referred to them as 'stout' lads who, in a voyage's time, would each be able to do the work of a seaman.[92] Four thousand apprentices were taken annually into the coal trade alone in the 1780s.[93] Henley's recruited apprentices from as far afield as Scotland, Ireland and Wales, as well as London and Newcastle, in order to overcome their wartime labour shortage[94] and even scoured the work-houses.[95] In effect, Henley's took advantage of the age and social vulnerability of working class lads to solve their recruitment problems; otherwise one cannot imagine in what they would be trained for as long as seven years. Of course, those sons of masters, apprenticed to their fathers, were in an entirely different category, being trained as future captains.

The length of the apprenticeship and rate of pay was generally related to age; a youth of about 18 would be bound for only two or three years and be paid at a higher rate than one of fourteen whose period of service would be closer to seven years. The pay of apprentices rose in wartime; in the 1780s the firm paid £25 or £30 for a seven year apprenticeship. This rose by £10 within a decade and by 1800 up to £50 was paid. In February 1808, Thomas Doyle of Kilride was bound by Henley's for three years for £55, to receive £15 in his first year and £20 in each of the subsequent ones together with £5 on his successful completion.[96] After the war pay scales fell back to around £30 for a seven-year apprentice-ship. They also received free clothes and victuals.

There was a higher incidence of disobedience among appren-tices than seamen on Henley vessels. Captain Robson of the *Polly* listed the misdemeanours of apprentice Richard Neal during a transport voyage to the Mediterranean in 1814–15. On 24 December Neal refused to keep watch and the following day became drunk ashore rather than help the ship into harbour.

On the 31st he was again drunk and rang the bell in the early hours of the morning. On 27 February he ran away with all his clothes but was found and imprisoned for several days. Finally, on 17 April he was caught stealing a large quantity of gunpowder and sent to prison.[97] In November 1814, two apprentices accused Captain Douglas of the *Freedom* of bad treatment and insufficient provisions. In response, Douglas claimed that they had sufficient food and were acting insubordinately. When one of the apprentices was asked to hold his tongue, 'his answer was if he held his tongue he would slobber his fingers'.[98] Recognising the value of apprentices, Henley's replied, 'it is no use quartering the lads have but a short time to serve they ought to be as good as men to us'.[99] Owners were aware of the favourable position of apprentices in the wartime labour market which is why Neal remained with the firm long after he was known to be unreliable and why Henley's recommended that Douglas treat apprentices with tact.

Apprentices were exempt from impressment[100] but this counted for little when there was a large demand for seamen in the Royal Navy. An apprentice might be impressed if his indentures were not on board ship. More pedantically, in September 1806 Robert Hay was impressed from the *Favourite*, 'owing to a mistake in his discription in the Protection was set down a mark over the left eye which should have been on the left knee'.[101]

As with many other aspects of their business, Henley's were able to benefit from economies of scale in the use of apprentices. When a ship had finished a voyage, or was being switched to another trade which required less apprentices, they could put the lads onto another vessel. Unlike owners with only a few vessels they would not have to pay apprentices for doing nothing while vessels were temporarily laid up or under repair.

Among other members of the crew occasionally used by Henley's were the second mate and the boatswain. Second mates were used in the Atlantic trades and sometimes in the Baltic. In status and pay the second mate was closer to the seaman than the mate, normally receiving 5s or 10s more than the seaman. Boatswains were sometimes used in the Atlantic trades. Finally, a cabin boy, who was only nine or ten years old and was not a bound apprentice, was periodically employed at the master's discretion.

The 'lot' of the English merchant seaman around the turn of the nineteenth century was precarious and uncertain. Consecutive periods of war and peace produced good wages and regular employment to be followed rapidly by unemployment and low wages. War also brought impressment, one of the greatest fears of the merchant seaman, indicating the poor light in which they viewed the Royal Navy in comparison with the mercantile marine. In general, most seamen came from the lower classes living around the coastal regions of the country. Their hopes for promotion to mate were based largely upon personal connections and their ability to transcend educational barriers. Consequently, most mates and masters came from commercial middle class backgrounds, often being sons of merchants.

From the owner's perspective, Henley's found the recruitment of seamen in wartime a headache because of their shortage and high wages, thereby creating delays and higher costs. Essentially, Henley's had no option but to pay these wages. However, through the agency of their masters, with whom responsibility for recruitment lay, every subterfuge was adopted in order to contain rising wage costs, especially by lower manning levels and the employment of foreigners, landsmen and more apprentices. At the same time, Henley's had to tread a careful line between these cost savings and the safety and legal considerations which such a dilution of skilled labour on board implied.

References

1. G. B. Hill (ed.), *Boswell's Life of Johnson*, London, 1887, 5, p. 137.
2. Some were recruited inland at places such as Manchester where there was no regular press. See S. Jones, 'Blood Red Roses: the supply of merchant seamen in the nineteenth century', *Mariner's Mirror*, LVIII, 1972, pp. 430–1.
3. HNL/77/8. From a sample of seamen Jon Press shows the most common age was 20–25 and then 25–30. 'The economic and social conditions of the merchant seamen of England, 1815–54', unpublished Ph.D. thesis, University of Bristol, 1978, appendix 17.
4. Conrad Dixon, 'Seamen and the law: An examination of the impact of legislation on the British merchant seamen's lot, 1588–1915', unpublished Ph.D. thesis, University of London, 1981, p. 22.
5. Press, 'Merchant seamen', p. 34.
6. This was very similar to the national figure whereby 34% of males

did not sign their marriage register in 1839. J. M. Goldstrom, *The Social Context of Education*, Shannon, 1972, p. 180. Seaman William Richardson, whose memoirs have been recorded, was educated and came from a family of good circumstances. S. Childers (ed.), *A Mariner of England*, London, 1908, pp. 1–2.

7. Crimps were middlemen who found berths for seamen. In a sense, they provided a primitive form of labour exchange but, in practice, often preyed upon penniless seamen. Press, 'Merchant Seamen', p. 83 argued that large-scale crimping did not develop until after 1815 because crimps would be impressed for encouraging desertion from the Royal Navy and seamen, anyhow, could easily find work. However, crimps were valuable for wartime owners facing manpower shortages or for indebted seamen.

8. HNL/114/28.

9. HNL/106/11.

10. R. Davis, 'Maritime History: Progress and Problems', in S. Marriner (ed.), *Business and Businessmen*, Liverpool, 1978, p. 179. This fits closely with the evidence of William Marshall who suggested 5 men per 100 tons in 1800. *Select Committee on the Coal Trade*, 1800, p. 48. Alexander Gray suggested the same figure for 1833, *Select Committee on Manufacturers, Commerce and Shipping*, 1833, p. 236. Although John Astle believed it had fallen to two men, *ibid.*, p. 415.

11. HNL/72/7.

12. HNL/123/4.

13. HNL/77/65.

14. HNL/59/74.

15. HNL/99/27. April, 1806.

16. G. Jackson, *British Whaling Trade*, London, 1978, pp. 76–7 points out that the American War of Independence and the French Wars set precedents for lower manning ratios in the whaling trade, especially by substituting apprentices for seamen.

17. G. M. Walton, 'Obstacles to technical diffusion in ocean shipping, 1675–1776', *Explorations in Entrepreneurial History*, VIII, 1971, p. 125 argued, for a slightly earlier period, that wartime privateering prevented a reduction in manning ratios. By the time of the French wars most vessels were required to sail in convoy so there was little point in hiring gunners to fight off privateers.

18. HNL/106/10.

19. HNL/106/16.

20. HNL/42/9.

21. HNL/12/7.

22. HNL/106/7. Moreover, at least five of the crew on this voyage were foreign.

23. For contemporary accounts of life on board see C. Garstin, *Samuel Kelly*, London, 1925; John Howell (ed.), *Life and Adventures of John Nicol*, Edinburgh, 1822; John Howell, *Life and Adventures of Alexander Selkirk*, Edinburgh, 1829; Childers (ed.), *Mariner of England*.
24. HNL/85/3. January, 1789.
25. HNL/77/24. December, 1797.
26. HNL/83/4. August, 1811.
27. HNL/77/57. July, 1809.
28. HNL/108/15.
29. HNL/55/3.
30. HNL/107/14.
31. HNL/107/14.
32. HNL/105/12.
33. Collective consciousness is a form of group identity whereby workers possess mutual interests. Seamen were conscious of their joint aspirations and acted in solidarity to overcome their grievances.
34. S. Jones, 'Community and organisation – early seamen's trade unionism on the north-east coast, 1768–1844', *Maritime History*, III, 1973, pp. 35–62; D. Bean, *Tyneside*, London, 1971, pp. 65–6; N. McCord, 'The Seamen's strike of 1815 in north east England', *Economic History Review*, 2nd series, XXI, 1968, p. 142.
35. See A. Aspinall (ed.), *Early English Trade Unions*, London, 1949, Letters 16, 104, 338, 339.
36. In addition to the above cited work also see N. McCord, 'Tyneside discontents and Peterloo', *Northern History*, II, 1967, pp. 99–111; N. McCord and D. E. Brewster, 'Some labour troubles of the 1790s in north east England', *International Review of Social History*, XIII, 1968, pp. 366–83; T. P. MacDermott, *Centuries of Conflict. The story of Trade Unionism on Tyneside*, Newcastle, 1965.
37. See R. Finch, *Coals from Newcastle*, Lavenham, 1973, ch. 6.
38. S. Jones, 'Community and Organisation', p. 42.
39. See McCord, 'Seamen's strike of 1815', pp. 127–43.
40. HNL/15/27.
41. HNL/15/27.
42. HNL/43/3.
43. McCord, 'Seamen's strike of 1815', pp. 139–41.
44. HNL/114/10. June 1819, Captain Gardner of the *Star*.
45. HNL/77/65.
46. William Richardson was impressed twice and on the second occasion wrote despondently, 'shipwreck and loss of all our clothes is distressing enough, but to be pressed into the bargain is really shocking; and I began to despond even to tears at my hard fate'. Childers (ed.), *Mariner of England*, p. 97.

47. C. Lloyd, *The British Seaman*, London, 1969, p. 157.
48. *Ibid.*, pp. 285, 289.
49. During the war scare of 1791, merchant seamen's wages rose to £2 5s per month, whilst those pressed into the Navy received only 19s per month. Michael Lewis, *A Social History of the Navy*, London, 1960, p. 10.
50. Including the company of criminals; see Clive Emsley, 'The recruitment of petty offenders during the French Wars, 1793–1815', *Mariner's Mirror*, LXVI, 1980, pp. 199–208.
51. Michael Lewis (quoted in Lloyd, *British Seamen*, p. 196) estimated that three-quarters of the seamen were compulsorily recruited to the Royal Navy during the French Wars. Lloyd, p. 196, suggests that the figure was 50–50 for previous wars. Also see L. Neal, 'The cost of impressment during the Seven Years War', *Mariner's Mirror*, LXIV, 1978, pp. 45–56 and Stephen Gradish, *The Manning of the British Navy during the Seven Years War*, London, 1980.
52. HNL/70/76. October 1799.
53. HNL/99/27.
54. HNL/82/12.
55. See N. McCord, 'The impress service in north-east England during the Napoleonic Wars', *Mariner's Mirror*, LIV, 1968, pp. 163–80.
56. HNL/94/8.
57. HNL/84/7.
58. HNL/69/20. April, 1791.
59. Public Record Office (P.R.O.), Admiralty (ADM) 106/1531. Promiscuous In-letters to the Navy Board, 1790–1801, 'H'.
60. *Ibid.*
61. HNL/63/27.
62. HNL/70/45.
63. After 1815 see Jon Press, 'Wages in the merchant navy, 1815–54', *Journal of Transport History*, 3rd series, II, 1981, pp. 38–52. For the eighteenth century, R. Davis, *The Rise of the English Shipping Industry in the Seventeenth and Eighteenth Centuries*, London, 1962, p. 134 suggests that seamen were paid 30s to 35s per voyage in the Newcastle coal trade. T. S. Ashton & J. S. Sykes, *The Coal Industry of the Eighteenth Century*, Manchester, 1929, p. 201, agree with this figure for the early eighteenth century, suggesting it doubled in the later decades. A. F. Humble, 'An old Whitby collier', *Mariner's Mirror*, LXI, 1975, pp. 51–60 drew attention to rising wages in the Seven Years War. There is miscellaneous material in the Parliamentary Papers, especially for the nineteenth century.
64. The Henley material, being a sample, may give a slightly inflated result of one trade compared with another. The selection of base years for the indices can be a problem. 1790–2 were used as the most

reliable pre-war years but even here wages rose temporarily in 1790 and this shows up more in some trades than others according to the fleet's deployment in those years.

65. Davis, *English Shipping Industry*, pp. 134–5.
66. Press, 'Wages in the merchant navy', p. 38.
67. *Ibid.*, p. 40.
68. David, *English Shipping Industry*, pp. 134–5 doubted whether there was any perceptible difference between the wages paid in various ports in the eighteenth century.
69. *Manufactures, Commerce and Shipping*, 1833, p. 399.
70. High wages might, in turn, keep vessels out of the coal trade and so drive up coal prices at London. Kirton frequently complained that high wages were making the trade unprofitable. They were also an important consideration in the passage of the Combination Acts, 1799–1800.
71. HNL/59/21.
72. HNL/106/3.
73. P.R.O., ADM 106/1532. Promiscuous In-letters to the Navy Board, 1802, 'H'.
74. HNL/15/3. This was confirmed by Thomas Richmond, appearing before the *Coal Trade Committee*, 1800, pp. 75–6.
75. HNL/105/12.
76. HNL/15/6.
77. HNL/15/6.
78. HNL/77/65. August 1812.
79. 37 Geo III c. 73.
80. *Coal Trade Committee*, 1800, p. 220.
81. *Manufactures, Commerce and Shipping*, 1833, p. 344.
82. For example, Michael Henley wrote in December 1793, '... we made a rule never to interfear with mates births if our masters was satisfied well otherwise they did as I thought proper'. HNL/105/21.
83. HNL/20/7.
84. Davis, *English Shipping Industry*, p. 122.
85. HNL/42/9.
86. HNL/69/31.
87. HNL/77/19.
88. During a voyage to Berbice in 1813, Robert Deas, the mate of the *Henrietta*, was demoted to seaman because of his inattention to duty and 'incapacity'. HNL/71/5.
89. HNL/87/2.
90. HNL/70/76.
91. C. Dixon, 'Pound and Pint: Diet in the Merchant Service 1750 to 1980', in S. Palmer & G. Williams (eds.), *Charted and Uncharted Waters*, London, 1982, p. 4 suggests that whereas an older seaman

was normally cook in the Royal Navy, the least competent seaman normally filled this post in merchant vessels.

92. HNL/69/35.
93. Stevenson, *Observations on the Coal Trade in the Port of Newcastle upon Tyne*, Newcastle, 1789, pp. iii–iv. Davis, *English Shipping Industry*, p. 119 believed that the apprenticeship of seamen was dying out by the middle of the eighteenth century.
94. In 1804 Kirton remarked that he had never known such problems finding lads. HNL/15/5.
95. It was common practice to remove poor boys from the parish rates by apprenticing them to a shipowner or master. E. G. Thomas, 'The old Poor Law and maritime apprenticeship', *Mariner's Mirror*, LXIII, 1977, p. 154.
96. HNL/28/12. B. Lubbock, 'Seamen', in C. N. Parkinson (ed.), *Trade Winds*, London, 1948, pp. 111–12 cites slightly higher rates than those offered by Henley's.
97. HNL/108/21.
98. HNL/59/102.
99. HNL/59/102.
100. By 37 Geo III c. 73 apprentices were exempt from impressment during the first three years of their indentures.
101. HNL/58/17.

6 · Profitability

How profitable was the Henley business? Like most entrepreneurs of their age, Henley's aimed at profit maximisation. Although their business expanded rapidly at the end of the eighteenth century, the notion of 'empire building' never entered their minds, though the greater security of a large fleet may have appealed to some owners. New units were added to the business only if they appeared likely to yield good profits. What did shipowners like Henley understand by the concept of profit and how must it now be expressed? Did they consider each vessel to be an enterprise in itself or did they work with the idea of an overall profit for their business? Moreover, did shipowners compare their profits with the capital of the business, its turnover or some other benchmark by which to distinguish high profits from low?

At the end of the eighteenth century, most entrepreneurs did not express profits as a return on capital nor did they perceive any specific relationship between profits and capital.[1] In 1813, Thomas Barnes, a shipowner for twenty years and an underwriter for fourteen, was asked repeatedly about the importance of the prime cost of a vessel in employing it but failed to appreciate the relationship between capital, freight revenue and profits.[2] Twenty years later shipowners responded to similar questions by expressing profits as a rate of return on the original fixed capital of the vessel; Henry Nelson, a shipowner, considered 10% a fair remuneration[3] and Henry Tanner, also a shipowner, 12·5 to 15%.[4] Samuel Cooper, a Hull shipowner, included working as well as fixed capital in his profit figures.[5]

There may have been a growth in the understanding of 'profitability' in the two decades after the French Wars, fostered by depressed conditions and the resultant need to keep a close check upon performance. Nowhere is there any indication that Henley's perceived a relationship between profits and capital although some ledgers are not extant. Amongst their correspondence, profits are only ever referred to as 'good' or 'bad'. In the accounts the profits of a particular voyage were occasionally noted though only as a nominal figure and not in relation to freight, costs or capital. Of course, precise accounting would be difficult in the shipping industry since owners had to allow for factors such as laying up, underemployment and the vagaries of the weather.

Nonetheless, Henley's surely possessed, in their mind's eye at least, a clearer idea of performance than simply 'good' or 'bad'.

The main guideline in estimating what was a satisfactory profit was the nature of the voyage. They would have considered £500 to £1,000 as good profit for a venture to the West Indies, £300 or £400 to the Baltic and £50 to £100 for a coal voyage to London. During a year a vessel might complete a voyage to the West Indies or three to the Baltic or nine or ten in the coal trade. In other words, she could make around £1,000 profit for her owner in the course of a good year, depending upon trading conditions and price inflation. Despite the existence of many of the assumptions of perfect competition in the shipping industry, temporary differences existed between rates of return in various trades before owners transferred their vessels accordingly. It was the owners with the foresight and flexibility of operations who were able to exploit these temporary disparities. Thus, Henley's gauged profitability according to the manner in which the vessel could be used rather than the amount of capital employed. A vessel had to be sufficiently adaptable for use in a variety of trades, thereby exploiting the changing fortunes.

Henley's would not have expected a newer, more expensive vessel to make greater profits. Indeed, to attain the same return on capital as an older vessel she would need to achieve a wider margin between revenue and costs. Henley's bought vessels according to their suitability in terms of age, size and general character. Although in a general sense they correlated prime cost and profit potential, their purchases were based more closely upon the ability of a vessel, within a particular price range, to fulfil the type of profit expectations outlined above. In spite of high repair bills, well-maintained second-hand vessels appeared capable of fulfilling the needs of their business especially in the bulk trades and were therefore more eligible than new vessels which cost more to buy and insure.

Most contemporary entrepreneurs had little understanding of an overall business profit or balance.[6] There is no extant evidence of an analysis of the firm's profitability at any period of Henley's existence. Joseph or Michael periodically remarked that their ships were doing well. Although Henley's could see the benefits of operating their vessels together as a single fleet, it may not have occurred to them, or they may not have viewed it as necessary or helpful, to estimate an overall balance.

There are no extant declarations of annual profits for the firm.

Sometimes a voyage lasted longer than a year or a vessel might be in the middle of a second voyage after twelve months. The profits of the *Eagle*, owned jointly with William Dodds between 1796 and 1802, were recorded in an account book in order to distribute the gains. These annual accounts were helped by the fact that she was mainly deployed on short haul voyages to the Baltic and in the coal trade.[7] A few annual accounts survive for the coal trade but these only lasted a few years and occurred where something unusual was being scrutinised such as a newly purchased vessel or a different port. Therefore, annual balances were an occasional policy tool rather than an integral and regular part of their accounting practices and future planning. Annual profits were calculated for the *Cornwall* in the middle to late 1820s.[8] This may have been an indication of improving book-keeping techniques or simply a case of looking closely at this vessel to decide whether she or other vessels were worth keeping in the worsening trade conditions.[9]

Information about shipping profits in this period is sporadic. Profits may have been falling between 1635 and 1770 because running costs and freights appeared to be falling whilst the price of vessels was rising.[10] Some profit estimates exist for John Long, a London shipowner, 1815–28, but are not fully authoritative because of the incomplete evidence and the fact that he had other business interests.[11] Disagreement exists as to the profitability of the eighteenth-century coal trade, suggesting returns of six to twelve per cent or more.[12] The Pinney House of Bristol was involved in the West Indies trade though shipping interests were entangled with their work as plantation owners, merchants and factors.[13] Profits from whaling were rising in the later eighteenth century and have been estimated at between 8% and 11% in the 1780s.[14]

Many contemporaries regarded the wars of the later eighteenth century as being profitable for shipowners. Robert Edington wrote of the 'immense and almost oriental fortunes' made in the coal trade.[15] However, the transition from peace to war brought many new features to trading with which inexperienced ship-owners were not familiar including the introduction of the con-voy system, the interruption of trade routes, the expansion of privateering and the wild and unpredictable movements of cost and revenue variables such as insurance. Record bankruptcies in the early years of the American War of Independence offset the windfalls made by other owners.[16] Similarly at the start of the French Wars, 'trade hear seemes to be quite at a stope of Acount of the falures hear and in England', wrote Captain Dodds from Petersburg in June 1793.[17] However, those with experience, business acumen and a fair share of good fortune survived to benefit from the large profits that could be made as the war progressed and freight rates rose.

The Henley material gives the best indication we have of the trend of profits. Following the prosperity of the American War, the shipping industry was depressed in the later 1780s. Vessels like *Holderness* struggled to break even.[18] This changed abruptly after 1793 when rising demand and constricted supply pushed up freight rates and profits. Henley vessels achieved high returns in the coal and Baltic trades whilst *Lady Juliana* returned 38% as a transport. Profits fell slightly during 1796–7, reflecting the reduced demand for transports. During the temporary peace of 1801–2 freight rates and profits tumbled; the *Lord Nelson* voyaged to the West Indies in 1802 but made a loss of 2%. War returned in 1803, exerting upward pressure upon profits. *Hermes* returned 4% on capital from a voyage to the West Indies in 1803 though it was several more years until substantial profits were again obtained.

A correspondence developed between Michael and Joseph Henley from about 1806, following the former's retirement, which indicated that their business in particular, and shipping in general, were both highly prosperous. 'I am happy to hear the good success of our shipping especially the *Freedom*s making such a good voyage ... the new ship you have purchased I wou'd not sell if she is a good merchantman as we cannot make more of our money than in good shiping.'[19] In 1808 shipping was expected to do well[20] but by the end of the decade profits began to fall as the government reduced their demand for transports. The change in the relative position of the demand and supply of shipping is illustrated by the fact that Henley's were now voluntarily offering their vessels for work in the transport service, whilst earlier in the war they had responded to requests from the Transport Board for tenders and had often fought to release their ships from the service after a spell. In November 1811 Captain Carter bemoaned the discharge of *London* from the Service during a trade depression.[21] In the following year shipping was said to be 'dull' at Gibraltar[22] and in October Michael Henley wrote from Tynemouth, '... things go badly here, trade dull & everything very dear the docks allmost empty'.[23] Profits were being squeezed from both sides; falling demand and rising costs. Henley's experience and expertise enabled them to survive this difficult phase; Michael was delighted in 1812 that they were still doing well.[24]

Demand continued to fall and at the end of the French Wars freights came tumbling down. Quinton Blackburn wrote from Newcastle in November 1815 that everything was depressed, '... Ship Owners will soon not be able to pay dock bills'.[25] The picture was the same in other ports. A business friend wrote from Hull:

... you cannot conceive any thing more dull [than] this place in every respect no business, the Docks are employed building merely to keep the boys at work, Carpenters, Sail and Ropemakers the streats are full all the docks are clear & not a single ship under repair ... I can scarcely get along the street for the Carpenters who are applying for a job.[26]

Reports from Henley masters at foreign ports, such as Hamburg and Amsterdam, showed that conditions were equally depressed there.[27] Although there were temporary improvements in 1817–18 and the mid-1820s, profit margins never returned to their wartime level during the rest of the period. Samuel Hall, a shipbroker, was expressing an accurate view when, in 1844, he said there had been a progressive depression in the shipping industry since 1815.[28]

A significant feature of the Napoleonic period of the wars is the declining profitability of the coal trade contrasting with the large returns in the West Indies and Honduras trades. *Lady Juliana* returned 48% on capital for a voyage to Honduras in 1807. Rising prices at Newcastle removed some of the earlier advantages of the trade but Henley's responded quickly to these changes by transferring many of their vessels to the Atlantic trades.

Henley vessels secured a high rate of return as transports throughout the French Wars. This is somewhat surprising since the guarantee of long periods of employment and compensation for capture should have made it a low risk form of employment. On the deficit side compensation for capture was tardy and vessels could be discharged unexpectedly at short notice or retained at a time when owners wanted them for other work.

Rising freight rates largely explain the high profits generated by the Henley business during the French Wars. Real freight rate indexes have been constructed from the substantial amount of statistical material in the firm's papers. In general, we already know that freight rates halved between 1640 and 1775, before rising steeply up to 1815 and then settling down somewhat above their old levels.[29] The Henley evidence gives a more precise idea of freight rates movements in the forty years after 1790, permitting an insight into real movements from season to season, year to year and trade to trade. Movements in freight rates were a function of changes in the demand for, and supply of, shipping. On the supply side, the principal variables were the net number of losses, the volume of new vessels being built, the delays caused by convoys and the degree of unused capacity in the form of laying up and passages made in ballast. On the demand side, the most important factors were the expansion of the transport service, the level of the harvest, the season of the year, changing fashions and popularity and the changing demand for goods of particular importance, especially shipbuilding materials.

Slow communications, the effects of the Navigation Laws and a degree of ship and owner specialisation meant freight rates varied on different routes;[30] whilst the real level of freight rates from the Baltic doubled between the mid-1790s and the end of the French Wars, those from the West Indies increased by only a quarter. Real freight rates for the importation of mahogany from Honduras almost trebled.

The French Wars exerted a critical influence upon freight rates, something of which Henley's and their masters were well aware. In October 1787 Captain Ladd of the *Peggy* had been offered a freight of fruit from Lisbon:

... but soon after there was so much talk of a war I was affrade to take it on board at Peaceable freights & I declined taken it on board till the Pacquet arrived to know if it was peace or war, she had 17 days passage two days before she arrived they Engaged a nother vessell.[31]

In May 1803, soon after the resumption of the French Wars, Captain Harwood wrote from Antigua: '... this rupture has not occationed any advance of freight – but should it actually be a War we will have some addition'.[32]

Figures for vessels gained and lost in wartime are incomplete though even if they balanced each other out, the supply of shipping would be restricted by the delays in condemning, selling and repairing prizes before they could be employed. Vessels were sometimes destroyed by either the captors or the captured crew. The conversion of mercantile vessels into naval use or as privateers further restricted supply.

Ships were delayed for weeks or months waiting for a convoy and then sailed at the speed of the slowest vessel. Sometimes convoys did not call at particular ports and therefore a fleet of vessels might be stranded there all winter. The *Lord Rodney* had to wait three months for a return convoy from Honduras during the winter of 1813–14.[33] Convoys, by 'bunching' vessels, caused freight rates to move in a volatile and unpredictable manner. The arrival of a convoy at a port, or even the expectation of one, would depress rates. In July 1801, freights from Petersburg were very low and scarce, 'as thier is a large fleet expected'.[34] Alternatively, the imminent departure of a fleet or a long period without a convoy could push up rates. The influence of convoys on rates was generally greater in the long hauls where only a couple of convoys arrived and sailed each year.

Wartime political developments contributed to freight rate movements. A large jump in freight rates from the Baltic in the first decade of the nineteenth century resulted from Napoleon's Continental Blockade which made trading extremely hazardous. The freight rate received by Henley vessels importing deals from Danzig rose to three times its prewar level. In October 1806 Henley's noted, 'ships are in great demand here since the Prussian ports are opened'.[35] Similarly, trading to Honduras became very hazardous because of the proximity of Spanish settlements and therefore very high rates were paid, rising from 65s per ton of mahogany in 1790 to 250s in 1810. Government action also affected the demand for shipping; the tariffs imposed on Baltic timber encouraged the development of the Canadian trade which had to be brought over a longer distance and therefore increased shipping demand.[36] The policy of opening up some of the long haul trades after 1815, such as to the River Plate, had a similar effect.

The season of the year affected the demand for shipping in some commodity trades. The demand for coal on the London market increased in winter as people required more for heating. At the same time, shipowners would expect greater remuneration in winter because voyages took longer and wage and repair costs were higher. An outward foreign sailing in winter might mean returning in ballast, as Henley's explained to the Transport Board in September 1809 on the subject of conveying coal to Anholt: 'This could be done on much lower terms in the spring of the year, the season is now getting very late this vessel very likely will have to come back in ballast.'[37] In a similar vein, Captain Dodds of the *Eagle* saw little hope of a freight back to England from Gibraltar in January 1797 since the season for salt had finished and many ships had sailed in ballst which would make freights at Lisbon scarce.[38]

The size of the harvest was one of the prime determinants of the freight rate from the Caribbean, particularly as vessels sailed from England before the size of the harvest was known. Charter-parties frequently included the clause that the freight rate paid should be the one current at the time of sailing from the West Indies. As a result shipowners battled with merchants from the islands to decide the freight: '... the shippers [merchants] ... say they don't think thay will have near enough to load me – but I think it is a pretext to keep the freights down, as there is plenty of sugars on the Island.'[39] In June 1812 shipmasters were paying merchants premiums of one guinea per hogshead of sugar and 15s per puncheon of rum because the crop was short following a volcanic eruption.[40] In 1813 another small crop was due the dryness of the season and the current freight had to be accepted rather than a prearranged one.[41] However, there were few complaints in 1814 when a large crop kept freights high. In 1815 peace and a smaller crop caused freights to fall. Not all vessels secured a full cargo. Captain Gardner of the *Lord Nelson* gained a complete cargo by calling upon friendships which he had built up over many years in the trade.[42]

A large and powerful firm like Henley's might be able to demand a slightly higher freight rate. However, a large measure of perfect competition characterised the shipping industry and it would be difficult to understand why a merchant should offer a higher freight to the Henley's who, though important, held only a tiny fraction of the freight market. It may be the case that influential owners found it easier to keep their vessels fully employed because merchants were attracted by their size and experience.

Sometimes a merchant offered a freight for a particular commodity which was out of proportion to that for others so as to encourage the master to load more of that good. In April 1805 William Burridge and Sons offered to freight the *Lady Juliana* from Riga at 50s per load for masts but only 40s for timber so as to ensure that most of the cargo would be masts.[43] In 1817 Henley's warned against carrying deal ends because they fetched only a low freight rate.[44] Shipowners had to decide whether to arrange a freight before the voyage or go out 'seeking' in the hope of finding a higher 'spot' rate. Henley's believed strongly in the former policy. In the light of the experience of the previous wars of the eighteenth century, Henley's probably took the right decision in arranging freights beforehand, especially with many vessels arriving at their port of destination together in large convoys.

The large expansion of the transport service during the French Wars, by increasing the demand for shipping, pulled up freight rates. The freight rate for transports was artificially controlled by the Transport Board and did not respond precisely to changes in the market, though to compete with mercantile ventures they had to offer a competitive rate. The rate paid at any one time could differ from the Board's official policy, particularly at times of special shortage. For example, the copper-sheathed *Alice* was paid at the rate of 30s between February and August 1814. The *Polly* was paid at the rate of 25s throughout the period 1808–15 despite a supposed reduction in the rate for coppered vessels from 25s to 21s in 1812.

Demurrage was another form of earnings for vessels and was a payment by the merchant to the shipowner for delays in loading or discharging the cargo beyond those days agreed in the charterparty. It had to bear a close relationship to freight rates because delays represented lost earnings. The best set of demurrage figures for Henley vessels is in the Baltic trade. In the years leading up to the French Wars the daily demurrage rate in the Baltic trade varied between £2 and £4. During the Revolutionary phase of the wars the rate fluctuated between £4 and £6. The same level maintained between 1803 and 1808 before rising to between £7 and £10 during 1812–14. After 1815 the rate fluctuated between £4 and £7, rising once to £8. Despatch money, the correlative of demurrage, was generally half the rate of the latter but there is no evidence of its payment by Henley's.

The period allowed for the vessel to load of discharge before demurrage was incurred was referred to as lay days, running days or working days. Running days included all days but working days excluded days of rest and holidays. Joseph Henley wrote in 1807: 'This charter and all such should be running days working days leave great roome for disputes.'[45] The wars complicated the system of agreeing lay days. Loading might be completed within the normal number of laydays for that trade only to wait another two months for a convoy. Therefore, charterparties had to take account of this fact in order to encourage the coincidence of loading and convoys. Charterparties in the West Indian trade frequently required vessels to sail with the first convoy to depart 60 days after the vessel's arrival at the port. If the charterparty simply stated the number of lay days without relating it to the convoys, the risk of delay waiting for convoy rested with the shipowner.

Costs also rose during the French Wars, thereby interrupting a long term decline in the real cost of carrying goods by sea. The secular decline in costs was explained by improved safety at sea, better shore organisation and more efficient vessels, along with a variety of subsidiary factors such as better packing, systematised navigational knowledge, extension of lights and buoys, dredging and steam tugs.[46] Costs were either of a variable nature, directly related to the voyages undertaken, or were fixed and thus incurred whether or not the vessel was employed. The main variable costs were wages, victuals, outfit, repairs, dues, delivery charges and brokerage. The main fixed costs were interest charges, depreciation, insurance and the various overheads of the firm. Overlap between the two categories sometimes occurs, especially for insurance, repairs and depreciation, though variable constituted the majority of total costs.

Henley's took great care to keep their costs as low as possible. Every item of masters' disbursements accounts was checked rigorously with a red pen and they were quick to reprimand insufficiently frugal masters. Cost accounting was made a good deal more difficult by the volatile movements in prices, both over time and between regions. In May 1793, Joseph Henley had written to the Navy Board asking for an increase in the contract price for delivering coal to the dockyards, '... as it is Warr and Wages & all other Articles of Shipping is so mutch advanced.'[47] After the war prices calmed down but the depression which hit the industry necessitated strict economy. 'I think I need not say anything about Expenditure the times must prove the need of attention,' Joseph had noted.[48] Movements in other variables during the war, such as exchange and discount rates, heightened the problems of cost accounting.

The trends of seamen's wages were discussed in Chapter 5, where it was seen that they oscillated violently and for much of the French Wars real wages stood above their prewar level. Wages were a major cost factor and so of great concern to masters and shipowners. During a transport voyage to the Mediterranean between May 1799 and August 1800, the variable costs of the *Lord Nelson* amounted to £2,261 of which wages were £688.[49] The *Cornwall*, on a voyage to Honduras in 1812, incurred costs of £2,076 of which wages totalled £641.[50] There are many other similar examples in which wages represented about 30% of variable costs.

Insurance increased substantially during the French Wars though never occupied more than 15% or occasionally, 20% of total costs. The effect of war on insurance rates is illustrated by the experience of the *Peggy* in October 1787 who was insured for 10% from Lisbon to England but to return 8% if no war was declared. The confusion created by the onset of war was explained by her captain: '... the low freights will not bear the high premin for if the ship should be in the Channel or as high up as Dover & war should be declared, they would expect the high premin as she was not in the Port of London.'[51]

Frequently, Henley's only insured part of the value of a vessel. The *Lord Nelson*, valued at £4,000, was insured for only £2,500 in 1801[52] and £3,000 in 1802.[53] Exceptionally, *Ann* was insured for her full value for a voyage to Petersburg in 1792, including the outward passage in ballast,[54] probably because she was a new vessel and peacetime rates were still being offered. Joseph Henley's remarks regarding the insurance of the *Aurora* in July 1812 suggest that cover for damage done to other vessels was rare: 'I would wish it inserted against all risks – doing or receiving damage provided it does not augment the premium more than

1/2 p ct but if they require more for the word doing please insure in the usual way.'[55]

With the exception of a limited number of colliers, Henley's put some cover on most of their vessels. This correlates with an estimate of 1810 that all but one-seventh of marine property was insured.[56] An anonymous writer believed a 'spirit of adventure' led many owners to forego insurance[57] though these were probably more speculative ventures. Only on voyages from the West Indies or Honduras did Henley's insure freights since here they represented a year's earnings. On her return from St Domingo in April 1811, the *Oeconomy*, valued at £5,000, was insured for £3,000 and her freight, worth £3,500 was covered for £2,000, both at six guineas per cent.[58] To the eighteenth century business mind, a freight was a less tangible loss than the vessel itself. Whereas the freight was the present earnings of the ship, the vessel was an important part of the assets of the enterprise. In most trades, except for longer hauls, freight earnings were worth much less than the vessel. If a vessel was stranded or captured, the owner's principal concern was for the vessel rather than the lost earnings which he would hope to make up on a subsequent voyage.

Most Henley colliers were insured in mutual insurance clubs rather than by policy. Little is known about these clubs except that they predominated in the north-east and consisted of ship-owners who each paid an annual premium sufficient to cover the losses of members. Stipulations were imposed on vessels in order to minimise risks such as that vessels sail in groups which possessed at least twenty guns between them.[59] In 1799 the *Eagle* was prevented by club rules from going beyond Gibraltar until she was sheathed,[60] whilst in 1812 a club known as the British Association insisted that the *Aurora* be supplied with 120 fathoms of new cable before they would insure her.[61] Nonetheless, this was clearly a cheaper form of insurance than by policy in those areas where it was applicable.[62] Sometimes, vessels were insured by a combination of policy and club cover. In 1805 Kirton's vessel *Providence* was covered partly by a club (£1,000), partly by policy (£1,800) with the remaining £200 left to his own risk.[63]

Vessels in the transport service were compensated by the government if captured. Henley's only insured transports against sea risks where there was especial danger. In October 1809 the *Lord Nelson* transport was insured because of the trecherous coast between Lisbon and Tangiers at that time of year.[64]

In general, Henley's only fully insured their greater risks or where there was a valuable ship at stake or if they could secure a cheap arrangement with a club. Otherwise, they might pay out more in premiums than they lost in vessels. Moreover, they were in a strong position to withstand heavy losses in a particular year and survive into more fortunate times, thereby yielding cost economies.

Victualling costs were closely related to the size of the ship and the length of the voyage.[65] Henley's accounts suggest provisions took up 20% to 25% of total costs. An astute master could make small savings by buying in provisions at cheap places and avoiding the dear. 'Everything is very hygh hear', wrote Captain Carter from *Memel* in April 1807: 'the Beef has rose to 9 pence pr pound and Bread 50 shillings [per cwt] i shall get nothing more hear then needs must'.[66] Before sailing a vessel would be fitted out with a good supply of salted provisions which was supplemented with fresh food when in port. Generally, fresh provisions were more expensive than salted, though in July 1798 Captain Grant wrote from Lisbon that he had stopped using salted provisions since fresh food was cheaper.[67] The amount of shipping in a port influenced the cost of provisions; in July 1797 provisions were dear at Lisbon because of the large amount of shipping there.[68] Convoy bunching caused sharp oscillations in food prices. At naval bases such as Lisbon, Gibraltar and Port Mahon, prices were frequently very high.

Henley's sometimes sent extra provisions in one vessel to another delayed somewhere expensive. In December 1812, the *Liberty* replenished her stock of provisions from the *Aurora* which sailed to join her at Gibraltar.[69] In August 1812, Captain Robson of the *Polly* wrote from Alicante, 'Everey thing is Varrey dear as the French Before we arrived took all the Corne & Cattle away.'[70] A vessel could replenish stocks during a long stay in a naval base by buying provisions from a 'man of war' but they might be of poor quality. In March 1797, at Lisbon, Captain Bone, 'bought Twelve Cwt of bread from the man of war at fifteen shillings ... out of that quantity three hundred dirt and dust'.[71] Certain places were notoriously expensive. 'Riga is the Expinsifist place that ever I was at', wrote Captain Omond[72] and several masters complained of high prices at Quebec. Conversely, Captain Robson of the *Pitt* remarked on the cheapness of provisions at Bremen and therefore bought in large stocks for the ship.[73] Decisions on victualling were sometimes taken by the master and at other times by the owner. One master blamed Joseph Henley for an incorrect decision: '... as such cold servear weather our Provisions have gone away very fast it was my wish to have add 4 more casks of beef but you did not aprove of it no doubt I shall have to pay for the provisions hear at very Extravent prices.'[74]

Repairs varied according to a vessel's age, her deployment and the weather conditions. Henley's owned an old fleet which they employed intensively and therefore the incidence of repair costs was likely to be high. Minor repairs were organised by the master during a voyage such as the replacement of minor sails or the purchase of some new cable. Anchors, major stores and yards were replaced during fitting out for a voyage. Major repairs were undertaken by a ship repairer, generally in a dock. Henley's normally chose Shields for repairs where the work was done to a higher standard than in London and they could rely upon Kirton's supervision.

During the 1790s the Transport Board calculated that the annual wear and tear was equal to 8s per ton.[75] Although it was obviously in the Transport Board's interest to underestimate this figure, it is nonetheless a long way from Davis's calculation of £1 per ton per annum.[76] Since major repairs occurred sporadically, it is difficult to balance them out between voyages and years to obtain an average. Davis also argued that repair costs averaged less than half this figure for vessels in the coastal and short sea trades, 'for many such ships repairs did not rank as major items of expenditure'.[77] However, the coal trade was notoriously hazardous and demanding of vessels having to sail in heavy winds and very bad weather and the constant danger of hitting rocks or going aground. Certainly Henley colliers were regularly repaired.

Betwen 1797 and 1803 the *Lady Juliana* had four major repairs costing £2,469. This works out at just over £1 per ton per annum,[78] although there were other periods when less was spent on her. A further £2,200 was spent on outfits of new stores.[79] Other costs amounted to about £12,000,[80] giving a total in the region of £17,000, leaving repair costs as about 30% of the total. This example exaggerates somewhat the importance of repair costs. Major repairs were undertaken during this period of six years which would not have to be repeated for some years. For example, in February 1797 she was repaired at Dudman's dock at Deptford at a cost of £1,080; this was described by Henley's as 'new top & great repair'.[81] In June 1803 she was resheathed and thoroughly repaired at Hurry's dock at Shields at a cost of £776.[82] In addition, she was a transport which meant high repair costs because of the demands of the service. If one were cautiously to advance, from the Henley material, a figure for repairs as a proportion of total costs, it would be around 25%.[83]

Port charges, dues, pilotage and associated charges comprised only a small proportion of costs, maybe 3%. Port dues varied according to the trade and the number of ports which were called at and varied from one port to another. In May 1808 Captain Smith of the *Pitt* complained about the amount of pilotage he was charged at Gothenburg and that as a transport his vessel should be exempt.[84] In the coal trade charges were high; it was a very short haul and there was a high incidence of charges upon coal including coal taxes which Henley's had to bear.[85]

Loading and delivery charges were largest on short hauls, especially the coal trade where much human effort was required to move a heavy, bulky cargo. However, the decline of the Tyne keelmen, replaced by drops and spouts,[86] and the use of cranes to load and unload ballast meant these charges were falling. They were also affected by the efficiency with which the vessel was trimmed. One master noted, '... half the day of Monday was spent in getting out one piece of timber it was rammed into the port and with the greatest difficulty got out'.[87] Sometimes when vessels arrived at their loading port, they were kept waiting for days by the merchant. Shortly before demurrage became payable the merchant would suddenly produce all the cargo within a few days leaving the master to hire additional labour in order to achieve expeditious loading. In August 1813 the *Lady Juliana* loaded timber at Quebec. During her first thirty days in port less than a hundred loads of timber were made available by the merchant, who then realised his error:

... and was obliged to give ous the cargo as fast as we could take it in to get ous load which obliged me to Imploy labourers more than I should have done and may say it cost the ship about 20 pound more than if I add got my cargo in a regular manner.[88]

This was a source of discontent amongst shipowners and masters and often resulted from a merchant giving preference to his own vessels.

Loading or discharging with river craft was more expensive than delivering directly onto the quay, but was sometimes unavoidable, especially during neap tides. In harbours with bars, vessels sometimes completed their loading in the bay outside the harbour which was hazardous as well as expensive; a problem Henley's encountered at Riga. Loading charges were sometimes high in the West Indies trade. In 1814, the *Trusty* journeyed to the West Indies and paid £530 in drogherage charges.[89] Droghers were small coastal vessels used to bring the cargo from another part of the island. Henley's response was to ensure that the produce came from close-by or use the ship's own boats. Another delivery problem in the West Indies was identified by Captain Douglas of the *Freedom* at Barbados in 1815: 'We are now unloading fast say as quick as thay usualy do here which in some parts of the world would be considered very slow.'[90]

Among miscellaneous variable costs must be included brokerage. The broker's commission was normally 2% of the freight revenue making it 3% or 4% of costs. Henley's did not always use brokers. They were most frequently used for transport voyages and in the later years when Joseph Henley was less active. Being major shipowners they were able to arrange freights without middlemen and contemptuously regarded them as unnecessary.[91] Gratuities given to merchants, officials and agents was another small item of expenditure. The Henley's bribed officials at Plymouth Dockyard in order to record a large 'delivery' of coal.[92]

Of the remaining fixed charges, depreciation has been estimated at 3% and interest charges at 5% on the value of the ship. Henley's, like most businessmen of this period, had only a vague notion of the concept of depreciation.[93] Certainly it was never mentioned in their accounts or correspondence. Overheads were only a minor item. Depreciation on their properties and the wages of employees need to be estimated and spread over the vessels owned. However, the allotment of such costs becomes complicated especially as these properties sometimes yielded their own incomes such as by renting the wharf and the bake house.

Movements in exchange rates were sometimes important. In 1819 the exchange rate at Christiania had fallen from eighty to forty-three dollars per pound over the last year and this doubled the costs for Henley's vessel, *Mary Ann*.[94] Discount and commission rates were important. While battling to keep down brokers' commissions, Henley's attempted to extract discount from ship repairers and other tradesmen wherever they could. Their size and influence meant Henley's were often successful in securing good discount. For example, they were given 10% discount upon the repair bills of *Lady Juliana* between 1797 and 1803.[95] Though Broderick, a ship repairer from Shields, had written in 1796:

I am surprised that you should request a discount upon yr bill at this time when you must know that discount is only allowed for prompt payment ... the terms of settling which is customary with all the docks in the river four months credit or 5% discount for prompt payment ... gave you an opportunity either to take the customary credit or receive the credit.[96]

In foreign ports, masters often had to pay commission on bills of exchange. Normally this was only a few per cent but there were exceptions to this according to such factors as the availability of currency. On an extreme occasion in Quebec in 1812–13, discount rates were 35% to 40%. Captain Darley had to pay these rates and on one occasion had to pay discount of £179 on a bill of £333 which represented a discount rate of 35% plus an error of 15%.[97]

Although Henley's were careful with costs, their shrewd business perception enabled them to recognise false economies. In October 1794 Captain Grant of the *Ann* was searching for a freight from Spain back to England. Henley's wrote to him warning that he must only load in a good harbour and not one of the many bad, dry harbours in the region, '... to go to ruin a new ship would be very bad conduct for the sake of a few pounds'.[98]

The movements in freight rates and costs determined the underlying or average level of profit in the shipping industry but the profit achieved by individual vessels varied considerably due to fortuitous circumstances, especially the weather, together with the quality of entrepreneurial decisions. The complexity of issues affecting the success of a venture is demonstrated in the following extract:

The day before I left Jersey I was offered a fright to go to Guarnsey, to load mahogany for Hamburg, I offered to go for 14s per tun if they wad give me a full ship they wad not ensure me above 180 tons I then offered the ship for £160 and two-thirds port charges, they wad give no more then £120 and no port charges had it been a littell soun our I believe should taken it, but if I had met with a long passage and catched the winter there, the people all by the munth I should have maid a bad hand of it.[99]

Thus masters and owners had to contend with such factors as the freight rate, the cargo size, wages, port charges, the length of the journey and the weather.

Weather conditions affected a shipping venture at every stage. Departure from port could be delayed for days, weeks or, occasionally, months by adverse winds or stormy conditions. The length of passages was largely a function of the weather as could be the rate of cargo loading and discharge in port. Even the availability of the cargo itself was frequently influenced by the elements. Finally, the amount of repairs required by the vessel at the end of the voyage would vary according to how rough the seas had been.

Colliers were often delayed at Shields for weeks waiting for favourable winds to sail down the east coast. In January 1796, persistent southerly winds at Shields halted sailings and caused the return of four brigs which had sailed a week previously.[100] As well as being time-consuming, sailing against the winds exposed vessels to damage. In October 1815, the *Lady Juliana* went north around Scotland from Liverpool to Shields, a passage which took thirty-eight days in adverse gales and caused considerable wear and tear on her ropes and sails together with the loss of part of her sheathing.[101] In November 1821 the weather on the passage to Onega was very severe, '... enough to tear a new ship to pieces much more an old one'.[102] Finally, in July 1817 adverse weather caused passages from England to Quebec as long as thirteen weeks when three was the norm under fair conditions.[103] Nor were vessels necessarily protected from the elements once they reached port. The most difficult part of any voyage was entering a port; a sudden gust of wind could throw a vessel upon the rocks or against another vessel in a crowded area. A badly sheltered harbour was often the reason for Henley's refusing freights. They avoided Lynn because: '... the Channel from thus to the roads is all dangerous if a ship should gett aground the sand scowers from each end by that means ships getts brook.'[104]

Transports were frequently required to make dangerous manoeuvres which, if combined with bad weather, could prove disastrous. In January 1797 the *Concord* was delivering coal on board the *Culloden*, man of war, at Gibraltar when heavy gales caused the *Concord* to be driven onto the Spanish shore and captured.[105]

Dragging anchors could pull a vessel into a dangerous position. The anchors were then difficult to haul up, leaving the master with the difficult decision of whether to cut the lines. Anchors were expensive and subsequent retrieval could not be guaranteed. In November 1807, Captain Grant of the *Valiant* had to take the difficult and expensive decision of cutting the masts as well as the anchors to prevent the vessel being lost on the Goodwin Sands.[106]

The elements also affected the loading and discharge of cargoes. Often the Tyne froze in winter as far as two miles below Newcastle, thereby forcing the cessation of loading at most staiths. In March 1811, Captain Gardner of the *Freedom* wrote from Kingston, Jamaica that violent winds prevented the droghers from working.[107] Climate could also affect the availability of the cargo itself, especially sugar and coffee. In November 1813 the *Aurora* was at Newfoundland and it was feared that she would not receive a full cargo because of the wet, foggy weather which had left much of the wet fish uncured.[108]

Weather conditions could combine with those of war to have a critical bearing on profitability. Heavy gales could separate and expose an otherwise secure and well-armed convoy, resulting in the capture of merchant vessels. This explained the capture of the *Lord Rodney* in March 1814.[109] Bad weather, by delaying the loading of a vessel, could cause her to miss a convoy by just a few days. In the West Indies, where convoys only sailed once every month or two, this could be costly and left the master with the difficult decision of whether to sail with a partial cargo or wait and load the remainder.

Among other factors which affected the profitability of a particular shipping venture were the character of the vessel, her deployment and the choice of master. These were all entrepreneurial decisions and have been discussed in detail in previous chapters.

The evidence indicates that Henley's achieved very high profits, especially during the wars, which enabled them to build up a large business. Any return on capital above 10% was good and this occurred often.[110] How far the performances of Henley vessels were typical of the industry as a whole it will be impossible to say unless other collections of shipping papers are unearthed. The existence of many of the assumptions of perfect competition in the shipping industry, especially ease of entry and the absence of market control, suggests a high degree of typicality. On the other hand, the line between success and failure in the industry was narrow, especially in wartime, as is confirmed by numerous bankruptcies. Henley's business acumen and the economies of scale of their organisation may have enabled their vessels to achieve returns somewhat above the average for the industry. However, the fluctuating level of returns achieved by different Henley vessels in the same period suggests that the influence of the shipowner was only one of several factors affecting the performance of a vessel and some other owners may have yielded similar profits.

High profits in shipping encouraged the growth and development of the mercantile marine along with the evolution of the professional shipowner. However, after the war, the depression in shipping, itself partly due to the expansion of the industry during wartime, may have removed some of the accumulated benefits. For the British economy as a whole high shipping profits suggested a large injection of demand into the economy. It is difficult to prove how firms like Henley's spent their profits. They are known to have invested in the South Shields Subscription Brewery but, in general, the avenues for industrial investment were limited before the growth of joint stock companies. Of course they ploughed back much of their profits into the business which stimulated economic growth by the impetus their increased demand gave to industries and trades associated with shipping. Even without proving that they invested directly in British industries, their profits were very important by means of the contribution made by shipping 'invisibles' to the Balance of Payments.[111]

A note on the profitability figures

The appendix offers as wide an experience, according to trades and period of time, as is possible given the constraints of incomplete data. Profits are given in a 'raw' form of revenue less costs since this is how Henley's would have regarded them; but are also expressed as a return on capital, both fixed and working. Fixed capital composed the value of the vessel herself, together with a suitable division of the firm's overheads. Working capital comprised such items as provisions and wages which were used up in the course of a voyage.

The prevailing rate of interest has been deducted in order to express the gains of entrepreneurship. Depreciation rates are derived from chapter two. Where insurance policies are not extant an estimate has been made according to what is known about prevailing rates. Even when vessels were not insured there was still a real cost involved. Expenditure figures have been collated from a variety of sources within the Henley collection, especially masters' disbursements and general account books, which has necessitated a painstaking task of allocating bills to particular vessels. More problematic has been the task of dividing the general costs of a vessel between each year in order to express annual profit. The incidence of major repair bills does not fall uniformly between years and therefore they are spread evenly over a longer period, generally five or ten years. The diverse mercantile interests of the firm until the 1790s presents further problems in estimating profits for these years.

References

1. S. Pollard, *The Genesis of Modern Management*, London, 1965, p. 235, observed, 'profits are distinct and are rewards of entrepreneurship per se ... the entrepreneur using capital merely as a tool for which he pays the market rate'.
2. *Select Committee on East India Built Shipping*, 1813–14, p. 57.

3. *Select Committee on Manufactures, Commerce and Shipping*, 1833, p. 393.

4. *Ibid.*, p. 399. In general, economists and businessmen alike would regard capital returns of more than 10% or 15% to be high. For example, R. Church (ed.), *The Dynamics of Victorian Business*, p. 37, believes a normal rate of profit to be 10% to 15%.

5. *Ibid.*, p. 470. This attitude of mind probably reflected the large outfit required by Hull's whalers.

6. Pollard, *Modern Mangement*, p. 212.

7. HNL/48/1.

8. HNL/43/76.

9. Henley's system of general ledgers ended in 1825. If profits were recorded in these general ledgers then after 1825 such calculations would have been made in the ship's own account book.

10. R. Davis, *The Rise of the English Shipping Industry in the Seventeenth and Eighteenth Centuries*, London, 1962, pp. 370–9, though he considerably qualifies this conclusion on p. 372.

11. Sarah Palmer, 'John Long, a London shipowner', *Mariner's Mirror*, LXXII, 1986, pp. 43–61.

12. W. J. Hausman, 'Size and profitability of English colliers in the eighteenth century', *Business History Review*, LI, 1977, pp. 460–73; Simon Ville, 'Size and profitability of English colliers in the eighteenth century: a reappraisal', *Business History Review*, LVIII, 1984, pp. 103–20.

13. R. Pares, *A West India Fortune*, London, 1950. He only discusses profitability in a generalised form and does not compare it with capital, business turnover, price inflation or other possible benchmarks.

14. G. Jackson, *British Whaling Trade*, London, 1978, p. 86.

15. R. Edington, *A Treatise on the Coal Trade*, London, 1813, p. 61.

16. D. Macpherson, *Annals of Commerce*, London, 1805, 3, p. 629.

17. HNL/92/12.

18. J. Stevenson, *Observations on the Coal Trade in the Port of Newcastle-upon-Tyne*, Newcastle, 1789, p. 7, complained of the losses suffered by owners in the coal trade.

19. HNL/19/12. Michael to Joseph, November 1806.

20. HNL/99/27. Stewart Omond to Henley's, July 1808.

21. HNL/81/20.

22. HNL/39/2.

23. HNL/19/12.

24. HNL/19/12.

25. HNL/16/3.

26. HNL/19/11. Thomas Rooke to Henley's, May 1816.

27. For example, see HNL/33/3 and HNL/43/3.

28. *Select Committee on Shipping*, 1844, p. 201.

29. See R. Davis, 'Maritime History: progress and problems', in S. Marriner (ed.), *Business and Businessmen*, Liverpool, 1978, p. 178; Davis, *English Shipping Industry*, pp. 197–8; D. C. North, 'Ocean freight rates and economic development, 1750–1913', *Journal of Economic History*, XVIII, 1958, pp. 537–55; D. C. North, 'Sources of productivity change in ocean shipping, 1600–1850', *Journal of Political Economy*, LXXVI, 1968, pp. 953–70; G. M. Walton, 'Sources of productivity change in American colonial shipping, 1675–1775', *Economic History Review*, 2nd series, XX, 1967, pp. 67–8. There is also freight rate information in the *Select Committee on Manufactures, Commerce and Shipping*, 1833, pp. 342, 368–71, 393.

30. North, 'Ocean Freight Rates', p. 540.

31. HNL/102/5.

32. HNL/82/16.

33. HNL/83/4.

34. HNL/99/10. Captain Robert Pearson to Henley's.

35. HNL/19/12.

36. Although this may have been slightly mitigated by the practice of bringing over to Britain vessels built in British North America, carrying timber as their initial cargo.

37. HNL/13/17.

38. HNL/48/9.

39. HNL/82/13. Captain Harwood to Henley's, June 1801.

40. HNL/82/37. Captain Chapman to Henley's.

41. HNL/59/89. Captain Gardner to Henley's.

42. HNL/82/37.

43. HNL/77/46. Masts were more difficult to stow and caused a slight waste of cargo space.

44. HNL/59/114. Henley's to Captain Stewart, August 1817.

45. HNL/77/53.

46. Davis, 'Maritime History', pp. 178–81.

47. HNL/9/1.

48. HNL/103/2. Joseph Henley to Captain Taylor, July 1816.

49. HNL/82/5,8.

50. HNL/43/4,6.

51. HNL/102/5. Captain Ross to Henley's.

52. HNL/82/9.

53. HNL/82/15. Robert Barry, a shipbuilder and owner, insured his vessels for no more than three-quarters of their value, whilst Alan Gilmour, shipowner, only covered two-thirds, *Manufactures, Commerce and Shipping*, 1833, p. 357.

54. HNL/34/1.
55. HNL/39/2.
56. S. Palmer, 'The character and organisation of the shipping industry of the port of London, 1815–49', unpublished Ph.D. thesis, University of London, 1979, p. 197.
57. Anon, *Late Measures of the Shipowners in the Coal Trade*, London, 1786, p. 5.
58. HNL/101/8. Alan Gilmour, John Astle and Henry Tanner, all shipowners, never insured a freight. *Manufactures, Commerce and Shipping*, 1833, pp. 391, 405, 409, 525.
59. HNL/48/16.
60. HNL/48/16.
61. HNL/39/2.
62. In 1809, members of the London Union Society, a mutual insurance club, paid premiums of 5%. To have insured colliers at Lloyds would have cost around 20%. *Select Committee on Marine Insurance*, 1810, p. 57.
63. HNL/15/6.
64. HNL/82/24.
65. Palmer, 'Shipping of the Port of London', p. 90 believes wages and victualling composed two-thirds of the master's disbursements. Two shipowners gave wildly varying estimates of victualling costs. Robert Carter believed the daily cost of victualling a seaman was 18*d*, whilst John Nickols believed it was only 1*s*. *Manufactures, Commerce and Shipping*, 1833, pp. 342, 349.
66. HNL/81/8.
67. HNL/34/25.
68. HNL/34/19. Captain Omond to Henley's.
69. HNL/78/3.
70. HNL/108/15.
71. HNL/105/34.
72. HNL/99/27. Omond to Henley's, July 1807.
73. HNL/105/6.
74. HNL/77/72. Captain Darley to Henley's, May 1815.
75. M. Condon, 'The administration of the Transport Service during the war against Revolutionary France, 1793–1802', unpublished Ph.D. thesis, University of London, 1968, p. 96.
76. Davis, *English Shipping Industry*, p. 368.
77. *Ibid.*, p. 368.
78. HNL/77/20.
79. HNL/77/21.
80. HNL/77/21, 22, 23, 26, 27, 30, 33, 35, 37, 39, 40. HNL/18/3, 5, 6, 7.

81. HNL/77/20.
82. HNL/77/20.
83. Davis, *English Shipping Industry*, pp. 368–9, suggested that repairs took up a quarter to a third of total costs in the 1680s but the proportion was higher in the eighteenth century due to falling wage and victualling costs. Of course, during wartime wages and provisions cost more.
84. HNL/106/18.
85. For a full explanation of the coal duties, see R. Smith, *Sea Coal for London*, London, 1961, ch. 12.
86. On the decline of the Tyne keelmen see J. M. Fewster, 'The keelmen of Tyneside in the eighteenth century', *Durham University Journal*, XIX, 1957–8, pp. 24–33, 66–75, 111–23; D. J. Rowe, 'The decline of the Tyneside keelmen in the nineteenth century', *Northern History*, IV, 1969, pp. 111–31.
87. HNL/103/2. Captain Taylor to Henley's, August 1817.
88. HNL/77/65.
89. HNL/119/5. This was 27% of total voyage costs.
90. HNL/59/103.
91. Smaller owners may have relied more on brokers. If Davis, 'Maritime History', pp. 171–3 is correct to suggest that many brokers were turning to shipowning, then Henley's may have had some justification for regarding them with suspicion, expecting them to put their own shipping interests before Henley's.
92. See *The Eighth Report of the Commissioners of Naval Enquiry. His Majesty's Victualling Department at Plymouth*, 1803–4.
93. Pollard, *Modern Management*, p. 240 believes most companies made no allowance for depreciation and simply charged renewals against revenue as they were incurred.
94. HNL/88/1.
95. HNL/77/20.
96. HNL/69/38.
97. HNL/77/65.
98. HNL/34/8.
99. HNL/70/5. Captain Kirton to Henley's, October 1786.
100. HNL/60/1. Captain Cummins to Henley's. In contrast, in September 1786 the *Pitt* completed the passage from Newcastle to London in only forty hours, HNL/104/13.
101. HNL/77/72.
102. HNL/89/16. Captain Sanderson to Henley's.
103. HNL/88/1. Captain Armstrong to Henley's.
104. HNL/104/24. Captain Dodds to Henley's, February 1789.
105. HNL/42/9.

106. HNL/123/10.
107. HNL/59/89.
108. HNL/39/2.
109. HNL/83/4.
110. It is becoming increasingly apparent that English industry generated high profits in the critical half century after 1770. J. R. Ward, *The Finance of Canal Building in Eighteenth-Century England*, London, 1974, pp. 87, 177 estimates that canal companies made profits of around 20% in the 1790s. F. Crouzet (ed.), *Capital Formation in the Industrial Revolution*, London, 1972, pp. 195–6 comes to a similar conclusion for manufacturing industry and observed that a substantial proportion of such profits was used for reinvestment in the firm, while P. Payne, *British Entrepreneurship in the Nineteenth Century*, London, 1974, p. 31 emphasised the ease with which good profits could be achieved in this period because of the buoyant market and some monopolistic advantages.
111. A. H. Imlah, *Economic Elements in the Pax Britannica*, Cambridge, Mass., 1958, p. 70 has evaluated the large contribution made by shipping services to the Balance of Payments. He shows that between 1816 and 1820, on average, shipping made a net positive contribution to payments of £9.92 million per annum. This was the largest figure in the eight items Imlah lists.

7 · Shipowners, entrepreneurs and industrialisation

The survival of the Henley papers has permitted an unusually detailed insight into shipowning and business techniques of the late eighteenth and early nineteenth centuries, an important period with the emergence of professional shipowning. The Henley experience also throws light upon macroeconomic trends within the shipping industry. This concluding chapter will present an overall retrospective analysis of Henley's business policies, techniques and methods, indicating in particular the ingredients in their success and the reasons for their ultimate decline, and evaluating what light the study throws upon the wider fields of maritime and economic history.

The coal trade was of prime importance to Henley's. They began here as merchants and then shipowners and it served as a backbone and pivot to the enterprise, steadying it in its years of development and expansion. It provided a reasonably steady rate of return on capital on a safe and stable cargo. The structure of the trade differed from others with the widespread vertical integration of merchant and shipowner. This offered Henley's some security against the wild fluctuations in freight rates, coal prices and shipping demand in these years of intermittent warfare. Also, it acted as a springboard for diversification as a result of the pivotal role played by many of its components. Colliers proved adaptable for use in many trades, whilst traders, repairers and masters employed by Henley's in the coal trade, now continued their business associations in overseas trades. Vessels filled gaps of idleness between seasonal long hauls with a voyage or two in the coal trade. Over the years Henley's increasingly exploited localised economies of scale at Newcastle which encouraged them to continue dealing in the coal trade and to apply these benefits, wherever possible, to other trades. Such economies included the employment of James Kirton, their Shields agent, as a virtual regional manager. They established a reputation as large, influential shipowners, for whose custom Newcastle traders competed by offering generous credit and discount terms. Potential ship buyers in the region knew that they could count on the quality of a vessel bought from Henley's.

The growth and development of the enterprise was financed principally by ploughed back profits, possibly backed up by Michael's property speculation and marrying into money. The expansion of their capital was encouraged by the profitable conditions of war and the absence of many alternative channels for private investment. The capital structure of the firm shows that some shipowners not only owned fixed capital in the form of their vessels but also as wharves, river craft and spare stores. The inability of historians to account for all these forms of capital has led to a substantial underestimation of the economic importance of the industry. Over half of Henley's capital was fixed in nature, thereby questioning the assumption that only in the cotton industry had fixed capital grown to such proportions by this period.

Henley's preferred vessels built along the north-east coast, especially at Whitby, Scarborough, Stockton and on Tyneside because they were sturdy and highly durable, frequently surviving for forty years or more. Their flat-bottomed hulls gave them great carrying capacity and made them suitable for lying on the ground at low tide for the purposes of loading and discharging cargoes or to undertake repairs or for closer inspection by potential purchasers. Most Henley vessels were of a medium size between two and four hundred tons which made them flexible between trades, an essential characteristic in the changing fortunes of wartime. Henley's also invested in prizes, constituting a third of their fleet, which, though less suitably designed, could be purchased very cheaply. However, they were suspicious of vessels built with ephemeral North American timber. The possession of so many foreign built vessels by English owners may have served to increase the dissemination of new ideas among shipbuilders, although this is difficult to prove.

The wars influenced the character of shipping in other respects. Speed restrictions in convoy put capacity at a premium over rapidity, thus further encouraging flat-bottomed vessels. The real price of ships rose during the French Wars because their inelastic supply could not keep pace with large increases in demand. Therefore, the expense and difficulty of obtaining new vessels encouraged owners to retain their existing vessels.

In the purchase and sale of vessels, Henley's considered both the needs of their business and cyclical movements in the ship market. Their experience of the industry enabled them to buy many vessels on a low market, especially just before and just after wars, and sell on high wartime markets. Ship speculation clashed, to some degree, with their interests in operating a successful and efficient shipping business. A strong, well designed vessel would fetch a good price in wartime but could also make a valuable contribution to the shipping operations of a firm. To some degree Henley's resolved this dichotomy by retaining their best vessels unless an exceptionally good offer was made. It was only towards the end of the French Wars that they sold out on a high market, fearing that a deep depression would follow the cessation of hostilities.

Having built up a sturdy, adaptable fleet of vessels, Henley's were able to send their ships into many trades; most notably coal from Newcastle, timber and shipbuilding materials from the Baltic and North America, sugar, coffee and rum from the West Indies and South America, mahogany from Honduras and transport work in many areas, especially the Mediterranean. The flexibility of their vessels enabled them to respond rapidly to new opportunities and achieve the most efficient combination of long and short haul deployment so as to keep their vessels at sea during the prosperous, though fluctuating, wartime conditions. Significantly, it was the emergence of these new trades, particularly across the Atlantic, that were not clearly connected with ships provided by merchants, that helps to explain the appearance of specialist shipowners like Henley's.

The firm's deployment policy changed over time; from 1775 until the outbreak of the French Wars vessels were normally in the coal trade; after 1793 they were increasingly used in the Baltic and the transport service. At the start of the nineteenth century a more radical change of policy occurred as they began to send vessels across the Atlantic, principally to the West Indies and Honduras, in search of high profits. Political obstacles in the Baltic contributed to the emergence of the timber trade with Canada. From the beginning Henley vessels were put into this trade which soon became a major area of deployment for them. With the return of peace in 1815, many of the new areas of deployment generated by the war declined, particularly the transport service and the Atlantic trades. In addition, coal, which had for long acted as a backbone to their operations, became less profitable. Their postwar policy was to spread vessels between the bulk trades of coastal coal and timber from the Baltic and Canada.

In order to take advantage of the flexibility of their fleet and the conditions of wartime trading, Henley's had to demonstrate entrepreneurial flexibility and a rapidity of response to new opportunities. This is most clearly illustrated by the speed with which they moved into the Atlantic trades when the possibility of profitable trading emerged. Moreover, Joseph Henley's constant involvement in the London freight markets enabled them to pursue such policies. Nonetheless, the firm was not adopting a high risk stance as a means of rapid expansion or quick profits. Instead, these imaginative policies were pursued within a carefully organised corporate structure designed to keep uncertainty to a minimum. The coal trade was the backbone to steady the business and this was reinforced by a judicious policy of insurance, covering the greater risks and using the cheaper marine insurance clubs wherever possible. In addition, vessels were regularly sent out with prearranged freights rather than risk the time and expense of tramping between ports.

Henley's also paid careful attention to the quality of master they appointed in the knowledge that he was solely responsible for the trading venture in the weeks or months the vessel was away from port. His wide duties embraced navigation, commerce, law, accounts and personnel management. The firm laid great stress on personal references and would initially place most masters in the coasting trades and then promote them to the more demanding deep sea operations if they were suitable. Successful masters became part of the firm's 'pool' of regular captains whose competence and loyalty were to be relied upon. Often they were paid retainers in order to maintain their attachment to the firm. Occasionally, Henley's shared the ownership of a vessel with a regular master; this was viewed not as a means of ensuring his loyalty but to expand the capital base and managerial responsibility of the enterprise. Indeed, disloyalty was rare, and incompetence was the principal barrier to appointment. It appears that the master's wide duties and responsibilities were comparatively poorly rewarded by Henley's. On the other hand, they displayed paternalism towards regular masters by finding them other work on retirement from the sea or helping out the wife if widowed.

The extension of such wide responsibilities to a paid employee, the master, was exceptional in an era when ownership and control of the enterprise were rarely separated. Some delegation of responsibilities was unavoidable and Henley's realised that some experienced, capable captains would shortly become shipowners themselves.

Otherwise, Henley's clung onto ownership and control. Almost all their vessels were solely owned and management was shared only within the family or with close friends, including James Kirton and Thomas Rooke. Even the masters who were given ownership or greater management rights were often close friends. Nor were the chief clerks of the business given much discretion until the contracting years of the business. As sole executors of policy Henley's were thus able to respond promptly and effectively to the rapidly changing sands of wartime, buying and selling vessels, switching trades, deciding upon a new master or choosing the type and degree of insurance. This was an agreeable situation while the firm was still quite small but by the time their operations had expanded to around twenty vessels, managerial diseconomies may have begun to set in. The huge archive of letters and accounts bear witness to the burden of administration during the height of the firm's power. Indeed, Henley's may have made precious little use of the accounts as a tool of future policy and long term planning, as the consequence of their reluctance to delegate a sufficient proportion of the more routine duties.

The appointment of seamen was considered the duty of the masters. Nonetheless, Henley's were keen to keep a tight rein upon wage rates and manning levels, especially in wartime when men were in short supply and their wages high. Apprentices and landsmen were used as substitute labour, whilst taking care to ensure that the vessel remained 'well and sufficiently manned'. Wartime conditions made seamanship more hazardous although the merchant service remained preferable to the low pay, long service and harsh discipline of the Royal Navy. Indeed, impressment was one of the principal fears of seamen. On the other hand, war brought seamen greater regularity of employment and higher wages. After the war their prospects were bleak with lower wages and underemployment. As casual employees they were never offered the company paternalism from which many masters benefitted during hard times.

Henley's close links with the government enabled them to secure regular contracts from the Transport Board. Sometimes three-quarters of their fleet was working on government contracts

period. No other archive has survived of sufficient detail to enable a comparative study. Henley's were one of the larger shipowners in London, and there were other owners, such as James Mather, with similar sized fleets largely under sole ownership, but it would be wrong to look for a 'typical' owner in an industry with such a diverse ownership structure. Henley's may have been one of a growing group of specialist or professional shipowners though more research is necessary to establish whether this was a general feature of the period. Moreover, one must bear in mind the very 'fluid' and changing nature of the term 'shipowner' in this period. Where possible Henley's have been compared with owners who gave evidence before parliamentary committees in order to show that some of their policies were not unique; other owners combined merchanting and shipowning in the coal trade, bought old vessels, were aware of the effects of war, took care to keep down manning levels and had a rather confused notion of profits and capital.

Some papers of John Long, a Woolwich shipowner of the period, have been unearthed.[1] Although a much smaller archive than Henley's, there is enough evidence to draw comparisons. Long was also a coal merchant with vessels in that trade. His vessels were second hand, built in the outports and bought cheaply in the downturn of the trade cycle. Like Henley's, he sent vessels to many parts of the world including areas where political uncertainty created the lure of exceptionally high freight rates. He took great care in his choice of masters and offered regular employment and ship shares to the better ones. There were also differences between Long and Henley which may explain why the latter was so successful. Long operated in the post-war years, 1815–28, when cheap vessels were available but were difficult to employ. His vessels tramped around in search of freights and had difficulties utilising cargo space. He also had business interests in shipbuilding and repairs which may have distracted him from his shipping activities. Long shared ownership of his vessels which led to policy disagreements with his partners, just the type of managerial diseconomies which Henley's feared. Long owned shares in only ten vessels and therefore did not benefit from such a wide range of economies of scale as Henley's, although he may have gained some advantages from his ship repair business.

What was the contribution of the entrepreneur, such as

Michael Henley, to the process of economic development in Britain? Ashton[2] believed the entrepreneur played an important role in the period of industrialisation. Similarly, Flinn claims more attention should be given to the growing class of industrious entrepreneurs rather than concentrating on the handful of inventors and their innovations.[3] Payne, on the other hand, wonders whether the good reputation of British entrepreneurs during the Industrial Revolution and the criticisms of this class at the end of the nineteenth century are fully justified, 'do the pioneers fully deserve their reputation for courage and adventurousness, progressive efficiency, organisational ability and grasp of commercial opportunity, combined with the capacity to exploit it?'[4] However there was no need for the average entrepreneur to be particularly courageous, progressive or adventurous to make a significant contribution to the Industrial Revolution. Robert Owen may not have been far short of the mark when he described entrepreneurs as 'plodding men of business'.[5] In fact, Payne is right to stress the cautiousness of successful entrepreneurs of the period.[6] Quite clearly, Henley's were hard-working though sometimes this was ill-directed on routine duties at the expense of developing a more systematic enterprise. On the other hand, Flinn and Payne do not do justice to the degree of business flair indicated by Henley's.

A form of 'ruthless conservatism' seems to describe best Henley's entrepreneurial talents. Ruthless because they were prepared to fight hard for the best deal with scant regard for any code of business ethics. Numerous writs were served upon them for failure to pay debts. They fought over the minute details of charterparties in order to secure as large a freight payment as possible. They were conservative because they were unwilling to take many risks, basing their policies upon safety and security. However, set within the context of the shipping industry during the French Wars this was the best possible policy. Fortunes could be lost as easily as they were gained in this period of high risk.

At the same time, Henley's manifested a strong tendency towards expansion and diversification. The movement from coal merchant to shipowner and the later decisions to diversify into the Atlantic trades indicates a good deal of business flair and enterprise. In fact, Henley's looked for a judicial mixture of constant, reliable trading, characterised by the coal trade 'backbone', and an element of development and change most notably in the Atlantic trades. Success depended on Henley's ability to keep a correct balance between these countervailing forces.

On the other hand, the nature of Henley's decline illustrates some of the shortcomings of British entrepreneurship.[7] The extent of the decline of the firm after the war is clear. Their fleet contracted from 6,000 tons in 1811 to 2,500 in 1815, a small temporary expansion was then followed by a further contraction in the mid-1820s to only 700 tons, just two vessels. The capital value of the fleet (constant prices) fell from £56,000 in 1810 to little more than £2,000 by 1825. Decline also took the form of entrepreneurial stagnation; an unwillingness to innovate and devise new business initiatives was reflected in their retention of the same vessels which they employed in a narrow range of trades. Only three were purchased after 1816 of which none was retained more than about a year. Responsibility was increasingly delegated to shipbrokers, such as Edward Rule, and senior clerks.

Economic conditions turned sharply against shipping after 1815 which helps to explain Henley's decline. Parliamentary committees confirm the prolonged post-war depression. Henry Tanner, a shipowner, remarked woefully in 1833, 'a man that has a ship of 200 tons and nothing else to depend upon is gradually going to ruin'.[8] The problems of falling demand and rising supply in the industry were exacerbated by amendments to the Navigation Laws in 1824 which served to undermine the monopoly position of British shipowners on some routes. Realising that a long term depression was engulfing the industry, Joseph began to withdraw his capital. Given his age and the severity of the depression, he achieved this with comparatively small losses. When Michael died in 1813, Joseph inherited £74,000 in the form of leasehold estates and the capital of the business.[9] On his death in 1832 Joseph left the larger real figure of £60,000.[10] In particular, he sold five of his remaining eight vessels in 1824, taking advantage of a temporary boom in the industry.

Many shipping enterprises survived these difficult years and one might have expected Henley's, with their substantial resources of capital and experience, to have 'weathered the storm'. In some respects their operations were more suited to the war economy. Their high profits were a function of a high wartime demand for shipping. Their flexible deployment policies were the consequence of wartime changes in trade patterns. They were able to speculate around the war-induced shipping cycle to buy vessels at bargain prices and sell them later at a profit. Their experience from previous wars gave them an appreciation of changes that occurred in wartime and allowed them to adapt their business accordingly. After 1815 some policy options were no longer open to them, yet there remained a large degree of continuity. They persisted as sole owners of a fleet of medium-sized old vessels used principally in the coal and timber trades. They continued to rely upon Newcastle for shipbuilding, repairs and commercial information. What ended in about 1817 was the policy of expansion and diversification which could no longer be justified in the poor trading conditions. Nonetheless, they operated a viable shipping business for at least another decade and in 1815 had even temporarily expanded their fleet and noted that conditions would improve once more in a few years time.

Quite simply, Henley's were typical businessmen with 'an eye to the main chance'. Previous experience stretching back to the Seven Years War told them that shipping tended to do well in wartime. They made some money out of shipping during the American War of Independence and by the later 1780s were waiting for the outbreak of war in order to invest further in shipping. Similarly, they moved much of their investments out of shipping after 1815, realising that the peacetime economy was unlikely to offer such favourable conditions to the industry. It is unknown where they then put their money although they never invested passively in London shipping in these post-war years. More likely there would have been investments in other industries or government stock. The likelihood that Joseph turned more towards government stocks is indicated by his advice to Quinton Blackburn, a business friend from Shields, in 1814:

I lay out my spare money in the three p cent Consols − should we have pease [peace] we may look to that fund to raise 20 to 30 p cent ... when the public take the idie [idea] for Peace from the great numbers purchasing will of course raise the funds − [if] there is a large loan wanted certainly funds will then come lower − that is all Chance my brother says the only guide he ever had was to count the buttons on his coat ...[11]

In other words, during the war, stock could be purchased at good rates since the government needed to raise a great deal of money to fight the war whilst, at the same time, potential investors were being attracted by other remunerative areas of investment, such as shipping. When peace came the government would need to raise less money and the expected trade depression would encourage people to transfer their money into government stocks. Joseph Henley's long experience may have led him to act ahead of the market and sell many of his vessels before the war ended and move his money into government stock before the price rose. Alternatively with the repeal of the 'Bubble' Act in 1825 there was more scope for industrial investment which is illustrated by the railway investment 'manias' of the mid-twenties and thirties.

Nor can one suggest that the business declined because their luck finally ran out. Although wartime shipowning was hazardous, Henley's were not especially fortunate. Their losses were no fewer than the average and their decisions were carefully considered in order to combine entrepreneurial flair with the avoidance of major disasters.

Instead, one may have to turn to personal factors to explain their decline. Family businesses rely heavily upon the interests and abilities of successive generations. This was particularly the case in an era when ownership and control of the enterprise was vested in the same individual and there was a widespread reluctance to broaden permanently responsibility for the firm beyond the family 'circle'.

The only likely inheritor of the business within the family was Joseph's son, Joseph Warner Henley. It would have been his responsibility to see the firm through these difficult years or to change the basis of the enterprise to something more profitable. Joseph Warner[12] was undoubtedly talented but never showed a continued interest in the business. After graduating from Oxford in 1815, he spent two years working for the firm in London. In later life, he referred to the value of acquiring a close knowledge of the shipping industry, and it is significant that he chaired several parliamentary committees on the industry.

He returned to Waterperry in 1817 and began to take a leading part in county and magisterial business, leading the life of a country gentleman. By 1846 he had become Chairman of the Quarter Sessions. In 1841 he was elected Conservative MP for Oxfordshire and held the seat until his retirement in 1878. In 1852 Joseph Warner was appointed President of the Board of

Trade in Derby's Government and also became a privy councillor. In 1854 Oxford University conferred upon him the honorary degree of D.C.L. When Derby and Disraeli formed a second Ministry in 1858 Henley was again at the Board of Trade. When the Conservatives returned to power once more in 1874, Henley was offered the seals of the Home Office but refused on the grounds of age and failing eyesight.[13] Although Joseph Henley had served the office of High Sheriff in 1817, the social achievements of his son, Joseph Warner, were considerable, lifting the family out of the commercial classes and into the ranks of the gentry or aristocracy. Indeed, Joseph Warner married the niece of an earl. Members of Parliament received no salary until 1911 and therefore relied heavily upon private sources of income. In effect, Joseph Warner used the fruits of the business to buy social promotion for himself and his family. Henley's were not unique in the nature of the decline of their business. The Gladstone family moved out of the slave trade into politics, whilst the Pinneys were largely forced out of shipping and commerce by the decline of the West India trade and instead invested in a wide range of portfolios engulfing cotton, canals, docks and railways.[14]

One of the central problems of British economic history has been to try and account for Britain's economic retardation, relative to other countries, from the later nineteenth century. From being the leading industrial nation she began to slip behind. Having supposedly exhausted all economic interpretations[15] for British failure, historians have turned increasingly to social and psychological explanations. It is alleged that the third generation of many business families were more interested in social elevation than continuing the business. They had been to public schools with the sons of upper-class gentlemen and wished to emulate their lifestyle. Martin Wiener has written of the 'gentrification of the industrialist'.[16] He argues that the middle and upper-class frame of mind, fuelled by a variety of cultural influences, had become, by the second half of the nineteenth century, hostile to industrialism and economic growth. Joseph Warner illustrated all these traits as the third generation of a highly successful business family who turned away from commerce and towards politics and gentrification.[17] However, his actions predate by nearly half a century even the date which Wiener places upon this development. When Joseph Warner was deciding to join the upper classes Britain had only just begun to industrialise. Consequently, the actions of men like Joseph Warner Henley could not cause Britain to fall from a position of power which she had not yet achieved. This suggests that 'gentrification' was a continuous theme throughout Britain's industrial history but its relevance as a causal factor in Britain's decline must be questioned. It may be that Britain was the leading industrial nation because she was the only industrial nation. Once other countries begun to industrialise the weaknesses in her industrial structure would be exposed and her economic performance would be surpassed by others. Principal amongst these weaknesses has been the social aspirations of the industrial middle classes.[18] Indeed, the legacy of men like Joseph Warner Henley continues to haunt the British economy in the 1980s.

References

1. Sarah Palmer, 'John Long, a London shipowner', *Mariner's Mirror*, LXXII, 1986, pp. 43–61.
2. T. S. Ashton, *The Industrial Revolution*, London, 1948, p. 161.
3. M. W. Flinn, *The Origins of the Industrial Revolution*, London, 1966, p. 180.
4. P. L. Payne, 'Entrepreneurship and Management' in P. Mathias & M. Postan (eds.), *The Cambridge Economic History of Europe*, 7, 1, London, 1978, p. 185.
5. R. Owen, *The Life of Robert Owen, Written by Himself*, London, 1857, p. 31.
6. Payne, 'Entrepreneurship and Management', p. 189.
7. It is interesting to note that even after the introduction of limited liability legislation in the middle of the nineteenth century less than 30% of companies survived for more than twenty years. R. Church (ed.), *The Dynamics of Victorian Business*, p. 36.
8. *Select Committee on Manufactures, Commerce and Shipping* (1833), p. 399.
9. P.R.O., IR 26/582/697. Michael's will was worth £125,000 in total.
10. P.R.O., IR 26/1292/380. These were years of falling prices.
11. HNL/16/3.
12. See his entry in the Dictionary of National Biography.
13. *Ibid.*
14. R. Pares, *A West India Fortune*, London, 1950, p. 331. Many Hull merchants achieved social elevation through local and national politics. G. Jackson, *Hull in the Eighteenth Century: A Study in Economic and Social History*, London, 1972, pp. 98–106.

15. On this subject see, for example, D. N. McCloskey, 'Did Victorian Briatain fail?', *Economic History Review*, 2nd series, XXIII, 1970, pp. 446–59; D. H. Aldcroft, 'The entrepreneur and the British economy, 1870–1914', *Economic History Review*, 2nd series, XVII, 1964, pp. 113–34; P. L. Payne, *British Entrepreneurship in the Nineteenth Century*, London, 1974, pp. 45–6.
16. Martin Wiener, *English Culture and the Decline of the Industrial Spirit*, Cambridge, 1981, ch. 7.
17. W. D. Rubinstein, 'The Victorian middle classes: wealth, occupation and geography', *Economic History Review*, 2nd series, XXXII, 1979, p. 621, argues that it was the offspring of members of London's commercial and financial sector rather than the north of England's manufacturing industry who were most commonly found in the public schools. However, in contrast to the Henley experience, Rubinstein found that most commercial M.P.s in the middle of the century were in the Whig/Liberal party rather than the Conservative. W. D. Rubinstein, *Men of Property*, London, 1981, pp. 164–6.
18. Of course, there was also a flow in the opposite direction, from aristocracy to business, especially in the years of financial crisis for the upper classes towards the end of the nineteenth century.

APPENDICES

Note: All wage and freight material is taken from the Henley collection. All wages are per month except in the Newcastle coal trade.

Key to wages tables

1. Average annual money wage.
2. Mean deviation of the average annual money wage.
3. Average annual money wage index with a base of 100 for 1790–2.
4. Average annual real wage index deflated against the Gayer, Rostow and Schwartz price index of domestic and imported commodities. Both the price and money indices have a base of 100 for 1790–2.
5. Average annual money wage index using moving three-year averages.
6. Average annual real wage index using moving three-year averages.
7. Average annual money wage index with a base of 100 for 1790.
8. Average annual real wage index deflated against the Gayer, Rostow and Schwartz price index of domestic and imported commodities. Both the price and money wage indices have a base of 100 for 1790.
9. Average annual money wage index with a stated base year.

Table A   *Seamen's wages in the coal trade, Shields to London to Shields, 1784 to 1827*

Year	(1)			(2)			(3)	(4)	(5)	(6)
	£	s	d	£	s	d				
1784	2	10	0		0		71	–	71	–
1785	2	10	0		0		71	–	–	–
1786	2	10	0		0		71	–	–	–
1788	2	13	3	0	5	6	76	–	91	–
1789	2	16	0	0	4	6	80	–	94	–
1790	4	2	6	1	1	9	117	117	100	100
1791	3	0	6	0	8	6	86	85	126	122
1792	3	7	9	0	11	3	95	96	165	156
1793	6	16	9	0	16	3	194	180	221	191
1794	7	3	3	0	14	4	203	185	206	168
1795	9	5	9	1	2	6	264	205	184	146
1796	5	5	6	1	6	6	150	115	154	125
1797	4	17	6	0	18	6	138	116	171	135
1798	6	1	9	1	2	9	173	143	201	141
1799	7	3	3	0	12	6	203	145	189	117
1800	7	18	9	1	18	3	226	134	164	103
1801	4	17	6	0	11	6	138	79	169	113
1802	4	10	6	0	13	0	128	93	203	147
1803	8	8	9	1	10	6	240	174	240	168
1804	8	8	9	0	16	3	240	173	225	152
1805	8	9	0	0	14	6	240	157	223	149
1806	6	17	0	0	15	0	195	129	219	143
1807	8	5	6	0	3	6	235	160	226	140
1808	8	0	9	0	7	3	228	141	221	131
1809	7	10	0	1	10	9	213	122	215	127
1810	7	15	6	1	5	9	221	129	201	116
1811	7	8	9	1	5	9	211	130	186	105
1812	6	0	0		0		171	93	–	–
1813	6	5	0	0	5	0	178	94	–	–
1816	3	16	9	0	3	6	109	82	103	71
1817	3	1	0	0	1	6	87	59	100	67
1818	4	0	0		0		114	74	106	74
1819	3	10	0	0	6	9	99	69	103	81
1820	3	13	9	0	6	9	105	81	100	89
1821	3	12	6	0	2	6	103	92	98	93
1822	3	5	0	0	5	0	92	93	–	–
1825	5	0	0		0		142	112	128	109
1826	4	0	0		0		114	102	–	–
1827	4	10	0		0		128	115	–	–

Table B *Seamen's wages in the Mediterranean, 1785 to 1821*

Year	(1)			(2)			(7)	(8)
	£	s	d	£	s	d		
1785	1	7	6	0	0	6	61	–
1786	1	9	0	0	1	0	64	–
1787	1	10	0		0		67	–
1788	1	10	0		0		67	–
1790	2	5	0	0	5	0	100	100
1792	1	10	0		0		67	68
1793	4	0	0		0		178	165
1794	5	10	0		0		244	222
1795	5	0	0		0		222	172
1796	4	5	0	0	6	9	189	145
1797	4	0	0		0		178	150
1798	3	19	6	0	4	9	177	146
1799	4	6	9	0	4	6	192	137
1800	4	4	6	0	4	6	188	111
1802	2	0	0		0		89	65
1804	4	6	0	0	2	9	191	137
1805	4	7	3	0	4	3	194	127
1806	4	10	0		0		200	133
1807	4	10	0		0		200	136
1808	4	13	3	0	4	0	207	128
1809	4	15	6	0	4	6	212	122
1810	4	10	0		0		200	116
1811	4	9	6	0	3	0	199	122
1812	4	2	6	0	3	9	184	101
1813	4	3	6	0	4	6	185	98
1814	4	13	6	0	8	9	208	121
1815	4	10	0		0		200	137
1821	2	5	0		0		100	89

Table C   *Seamen's wages in the Baltic, 1786 to 1829*

Year	(1)			(2)		(3)	(4)	(5)	(6)
	£	s	d	s	d				
1786	1	11	3	1	3	58	–	56	–
1787	1	10	0	0		56	–	58	–
1788	1	9	6	0	6	55	–	–	–
1789	1	14	8	0	5	64	–	97	–
1790	3	3	0	0		117	117	100	100
1791	2	19	6	0	6	111	110	105	102
1792	1	18	10	3	0	72	73	131	122
1793	3	12	0	6	5	133	123	170	147
1794	5	0	6	6	6	187	170	188	153
1795	5	2	6	2	6	191	148	184	146
1796	4	19	6	0	10	185	142	–	–
1797	4	15	0	0		177	149	–	–
1799	4	19	10	7	11	186	133	191	119
1800	5	2	6	2	6	191	113	–	–
1801	5	5	0	0		195	112	–	–
1803	4	17	0	9	7	180	130	194	135
1804	5	12	6	6	0	209	150	199	135
1805	5	3	6	11	10	193	126	190	126
1806	5	5	0	0		195	129	184	120
1807	4	17	6	6	3	181	123	171	107
1808	4	14	0	4	10	175	108	173	102
1809	4	5	0	5	0	158	91	170	101
1810	5	0	0	0		186	108	167	97
1811	4	10	0	0		167	103	159	90
1812	4	0	0	0		149	81	150	82
1813	4	6	8	4	1	161	85	153	91
1814	3	14	8	12	3	139	81	129	86
1815	4	5	0	5	0	158	108	108	76
1816	2	8	7	2	0	90	68	87	60
1817	2	1	0	1	10	76	51	88	59
1818	2	10	6	1	11	95	61	91	64
1819	2	11	3	3	9	95	66	90	71
1820	2	5	0	5	0	84	65	90	80
1821	2	9	4	1	0	92	82	93	87
1822	2	10	0	0		93	94	99	92
1823	2	10	0	0		93	85	106	90
1824	3	0	0	0		112	98	112	95
1825	3	0	0	0		112	88	107	92
1826	3	0	0	0		112	100	104	94
1827	2	12	6	2	6	98	88	101	92
1828	2	15	0	0		102	94	–	–
1829	2	15	0	0		102	95	–	–

Table D   *Seamen's wages in the Canadian timber trade, 1787 to 1828*

Year	(1)			(2)		(9)
	£	s	d	s	d	
1787	1	1	0	0		100
1808	5	0	0	0		476
1810	4	15	0	5	0	452
1812	4	16	6	4	6	460
1813	4	10	0	10	0	429
1814	5	0	0	0		476
1815	3	0	0	0		286
1817	2	0	0	0		191
1818	2	10	0	2	0	238
1819	2	15	0	0		262
1820	2	10	6	0	9	240
1821	2	10	0	0		238
1822	2	10	0	0		238
1823	2	10	0	0		238
1824	3	0	0	0		286
1826	2	15	0	0		262
1828	2	15	0	0		262

Note   [a] Index with a base of 100 for 1787

Table E   *Seamen's wages in the West Indies trade, 1789 to 1823*

Year	(1)			(2)		(9)
	£	s	d	s	d	
1789	1	9	0	1	0	100
1793	4	0	0	0		276
1794	4	0	0	0		276
1795	4	5	0	5	0	293
1801	4	5	0	5	0	293
1802	2	5	0	5	0	155
1803	3	3	0	0		217
1804	4	10	0	0		310
1809	4	10	0	0		310
1810	4	10	0	0		310
1811	4	0	0	0		276
1812	4	0	0	0		276
1813	4	10	0	0		310
1814	3	15	0	0		259
1815	3	0	0	0		207
1816	2	5	0	5	0	155
1818	2	0	0	0		138
1819	2	5	0	0		155
1823	2	10	0	0		172

Note   [a] Index base of 100 for 1789

Table F   *Seamen's wages in the Honduras mahogany trade, 1790 to 1816*

Year	(1)			(2)		(7)	(8)
	£	s	d	s	d		
1790	1	15	0	0	0	100	100
1801	3	0	0	0	0	171	98
1802	2	0	0	0	0	114	83
1803	4	10	0	0	0	257	186
1804	4	10	0	0	0	257	185
1805	4	10	0	0	0	257	168
1806	4	10	0	0	0	257	170
1807	4	11	3	1	9	261	178
1809	4	10	0	0	0	257	148
1810	4	15	0	0	0	271	158
1811	4	10	0	0	0	257	158
1812	4	6	9	4	6	247	135
1813	4	15	0	5	0	271	143
1814	3	10	0	0	0	200	116
1815	2	10	0	0	0	143	98
1816	1	5	0	0	0	129	97

Table G   *Seamen's wages to South America, 1806–13*

Year	(1)			(2)	
	£	s	d	s	d
1806	4	10	0	0	0
1807	4	10	0	0	0
1811	4	0	0	0	0
1812	4	0	0	0	0
1813	4	7	6	2	6

Table H *Freight rates for deal from St. Petersburg, 1789 to 1829*

Year	Deals [a]	Money freight rate index [1790 – 2 = 100]	Real freight rate [b]
1789	50	88	–
1790	60	106	106
1791	63	110	109
1792	48	84	85
1793	95	168	155
1794	70	124	111
1796	100	176	136
1800	140	247	146
1801	155	274	157
1806	120	212	140
1814	230	407	236
1815	180	318	218
1816	78	137	102
1817	75	133	90
1818	113	199	128
1820	75	133	102
1821	71	125	111
1822	78	138	140
1823	86	152	139
1826	75	133	118
1827	65	115	103
1829	70	124	115

Notes

[a] Shillings per Petersburg standard hundred.

[b] Real freight rate index deflated against Gayer, Rostow and Schwartz price index of domestic and imported commodities. Base of 100 for 1790–2.

Table I   *Freight rates from Honduras 1790 to 1826*

Date	Mahogany [a]	Logwood [a]	Money index of mahogany freight rates [1790 = 100]	Real index of mahogany freight rates [b]
1790	65	35	100	100
1791	105	45	162	161
1801	120	80	185	106
1802	113	63	173	126
1803	252	168	388	280
1804	260	130	400	287
1805	225	113	347	228
1806	225	113	347	230
1807	205	105	316	215
1808	220	110	339	210
1810	250	120	385	224
1811	225	113	347	213
1812	189	103	291	156
1813	252	126	388	205
1814	210	105	323	184
1815	140	70	216	149
1816	100	50	154	116
1819	100	50	154	107
1826	90	–	139	124

Notes

[a] Shillings per ton.

[b] Base of 100 for 1790, deflated against Gayer, Rostow and Schwartz price index of domestic and imported commodities.

Table J *Freight rates in the transport service, 1775 to 1822*
(shillings per ton per month)

Date	Unsheathed	Wooden sheathed	Copper sheathed
1775–83	11–12	11–12	11–12
1783	10	10	10
1787	8	–	–
1789	8	–	–
1790	11	–	–
1793	12–13	12–13	12–13
1794/5	13	–	–
1796	13	15	15
1798	13	13	15
1799	13	15	16
1800	16	18	20
1802	12	12	12
1803	–	17–18	20
1804–7	–	17	19
Apr 1807	15	19	25
1809–13	18–20	21	21–25
1813–15	–	20	–
1814	–	–	30
Oct 1815	–	–	19
1818–19	–	–	16
1820–22	–	–	13

Source: Some of this material on Henley vessels was taken from P.R.O.
ADM 108/148–67, Ships and Freight Ledgers. Confirmatory
evidence relating to non-Henley vessels can also be found here.

Table K   *Freight rates on sugar from the West Indies,*
1795 to 1818

Year	Sugar [a]		Money freight rate [1795 = 100]	Real freight rate [b]
	s	d		
1795	6	0	100	100
1801	9	6	159	117
1802	5	0	84	79
1803	4	6	75	70
1810	10	0	167	125
1812	9	0	150	106
1813	9	0	150	102
1814	9	6	159	116
1815	8	0	134	119
1816	5	6	92	90
1817	4	6	75	66
1818	4	6	75	62

Notes
[a] Shillings per cwt.
[b] Real freight rate index deflated against Gayer, Rostow and Schwartz price index of domestic and imported commodities. Base of 100 for 1795.

Table L   *Freight rates from Quebec, 1808–28*

Date	Deals [a]	Timber [b]	Masts
	s	s	s
1808	240	110	120
1810	410	160	170
1812	240	115	125
1813	240	115	–
1817	125	50	55
1818	175	–	–
1819	195	65	65
1820	125	50	55
1821	130	42	–
1822	140	43	46
1823	150	50	–
1826	140	45	50
1828	120	40	–

Notes
[a] Per Petersburg standard hundred.
[b] Per load of oak timber.

Table M *Demurrage rates in various trades, 1786 to 1828*
(Pounds per day)

Date	Baltic	Canada	West Indies	Honduras	Mediter-ranean	Transport
	£	£	£	£	£	£
1786	3	–	–	–	–	–
1787	3	–	–	–	–	–
1788	2	–	–	–	2	4
	3	–	–	–	–	–
1789	3	–	–	–	–	–
1790	4	–	–	4	–	–
1791	2	–	–	–	–	–
	4	–	–	–	–	–
1792	2	–	–	–	–	–
	4	–	–	–	–	–
1793	4	–	–	–	–	–
	5	–	–	–	–	–
1794	4	–	–	–	–	4
1795	5	–	–	–	–	4–5
1796	5–6	–	–	–	–	2
1797	5	–	–	–	–	–
1800	5	–	–	–	–	4
1801	–	–	–	5	–	–
1802	–	–	–	4	–	–
1803	5	–	–	10	–	–
1804	4–6	–	–	8	–	–
1805	5–6	–	–	8	–	–
1806	6	–	–	10	–	–
1807	5–6	–	–	8	–	–
1808	4	5	–	8	7	–
1809	–	–	7	–	6	–
1810	–	8–10	7–10	8	–	–
1811	–	8	7	10	3	6
1812	8–10	8	7	10–12	–	–
1813	7	–	7	10–12	6	–
	–	–	–	–	7	–
1814	10	–	–	10	–	–
1815	5	10	–	10	–	–
1816	5–7	–	–	10	–	–
1817	4–8	6–7	–	–	–	–
1818	4–6	5–7	–	–	–	–
1819	5–6	5–6	–	–	–	–
1820	6	5–6	–	–	–	–
1821	6–7	6–7	–	–	–	–
1822	–	6	–	–	–	–
1823	–	5–6	–	–	–	–
1826	–	6	–	–	–	–
1828	5	–	–	–	–	–

Table N   *Profit and loss of selected vessels, 1792–1829*

Date	Deployment	Annual Profit (£)	Annual Profit (% of capital)
Adelphi, 1810–11			
1810–11	1 Tspt.	251	6
Cornwall, 1810–31			
1812	Honduras	2,413	39
1813	St. Kitts	879	14
1814	St. Kitts	2,525	40
1815	Honduras and 1 c.v.	2,990	43
1816	1 Bal., 3 c.v.	90	1
1817	3 Bal.	124	2
1818	1 Can., 1 Bal.	495	10
1819	1 Can., 1 Bal.	317	6
1820	1 Can., 1 Bal.	−298	5 loss
1821	1 Can., 1 Bal.	102	2
1822	1 Can., 1 Bal.	259	5
1823	2 Can., 1 c.v.	808	13
1824	1 Can., 1 Bal.	−136	2 loss
1825	2 Bal.	279	5
1826	1 Can., 1 c.v.	−148	3 loss
1828	1 Can., 2 c.v.	2	0
1829	2 Bal.	28	1
Echo, 1803–4			
1803–4	8 c.v.	525	11
Elizabeth, 1810–11			
1810–11	1 Tspt.	639	17
Europa, 1810–13			
1811–12	1 Tspt.	404	15
Favourite, 1803–6			
1804	6 c.v.	−369	5 loss
1805	2 c.v., 2 Bal., 1 Tspt.	658	13
1806	4 c.v.	6	0
George, 1800			
1800	8 c.v.	280	9

Table N continued

Date	Deployment	Annual Profit (£)	Annual Profit (% of capital)
Hermes, 1802–5			
1803	Jamaica	149	4
1804	Jamaica	Profit much higher though full cost figures not extant.	
Lady Juliana, 1791–1825			
1792–3	1 Bal., 3 c.v.	−159	3 loss
1793–1802	Tspt.	1,363	38
1803	1 Bal., repairs	351	11
1804	2 Bal., repairs	−575	15 loss
1805–6	1 Bal., 1 c.v., 1 Tspt.	176	4
1807	Honduras	2,004	48
1808	1 Can., 1 c.v.	1,423	33
1809–11	1 Tspt.	1,410	33
1812	1 Can.	1,738	53
1813	1 Can., 2 c.v.	1,959	35
1814	1 Bal., 1 c.v.	1,824	44
(Includes £1,000 for a cancelled charterparty. Without this, return of 20%)			
1815	1 Can., 1 c.v.	1,183	31
1816	1 Bal.	−254	13 loss
1817	3 Bal.	365	14
1818	2 Bal.	331	10
1819	1 c.v.	−197	8 loss
1820	1 Can.	425	16
1821	1 Can., 1 Bal., 1 c.v.	−183	5 loss
1822	1 Can.	196	8
1823	1 Can., 1 Bal., 1 c.v.	886	23
1824	1 Can., 1 Bal.	174	5
Lord Nelson, 1799–1824			
1799	2 c.v.	2,418	22
1799–1800	Tspt.	2,324	43
1800–1	1 Bal.	688	12
1801	Antigua	1,240	24

Table N continued

Date	Deployment	Annual Profit (£)	Annual Profit (% of capital)
1802	Antigua	− 83	2 loss
1802−3	Gibraltar and Antigua	− full details not available but profits still low.	
1804	3 c.v., 1 Bal.	−267	4 loss
1805	Tspt.	116	2
1806	1 Bal.	−420	6 loss
1806−11	Tspt.	1,690	28
1813−14	Honduras	1,566	26
1814	1 Bal.	822	13
1815	St. Vincent	1,349	25
1816	St. Vincent, 2 c.v.	638	10
1817	3 Bal., 2 c.v.	172	3
1818	3 Bal., 2 c.v.	362	6
1819	1 Bal., 3 c.v.	212	3
1820	4 c.v., 1 Can.	−63	1 loss
1821	2 c.v., 1 Can., 1 Bal.	89	2
1822	2 c.v., 1 Can.	−30	1 loss
1823	1 Can., 2 Bal.	328	6
Ocean, 1801−2			
1801−2	11 c.v.	−398	7 loss
Pitt, 1804−10			
1804	3 c.v.	54	2
1806	4 c.v., 1 Tspt.	1,129	15
1807	1 Bal., 2 c.v.	944	13
1807−9	Tspt.	1,673	32
Polly, 1805−24			
1805−8	Tspt.	1,003	19
1808−15	Tspt.	2,125	40
1816	1 c.v., 1 Bal.	−341	7 loss
1817	3 c.v., 2 Bal.	250	4
1818	5 c.v., 2 Bal.	699	9
1819	1 c.v., 1 Bal., 1 Can.	432	8

Table N continued

Date	Deployment	Annual Profit (£)	Annual Profit (% of capital)
Salus, 1807–11			
1807–11	Tspt.	1,628	35
Surry, 1806–10			
1807	Surinam	1,999	40
1808	Honduras	1,627	35
1809	Honduras	1,979	42
1810	St. Vincent	1,336	30

Note

c.v.   = Coal voyage
Can.   = Canada
Bal.   = Baltic
Tspt. = Transport service

Vessel dates refer to period of ownership by Henley's. Figures still refer to annual profit when voyage is spread over several years.

Table O   *Profit and loss by year of selected vessels, 1792 to 1829*

Date	Annual Profit (£)	Annual Profit (% of capital)
1792–3		
Lady Juliana	−159	3 loss
1794–8		
Lady Juliana	1,363	38
1799		
Lady Juliana	1,363	38
Lord Nelson (1799–1800)	2,324	43
1800		
Lord Nelson (1800–1)	688	12
George	280	9
Lady Juliana	1,363	38
1801		
Lady Juliana	1,363	38
Lord Nelson	1,240	24
Ocean (1801–2)	−398	7 loss
1802		
Lady Juliana	1,363	38
Lord Nelson	−83	2 loss
1803		
Echo (1803–4)	525	11
Hermes	149	4
Lady Juliana	351	11
Lord Nelson	Low	Low
1804		
Pitt	54	2
Favourite	−369	5 loss
Hermes	High	High
Lady Juliana	−575	15 loss
Lord Nelson	−267	4 loss
1805		
Favourite	658	13
Lady Juliana (1805–6)	176	4
Lord Nelson	116	2
Polly	1,003	19
1806		
Favourite	6	0
Lord Nelson	−420	6 loss
Pitt	1,129	15
Polly	1,003	19

Table O continued

Date	Annual Profit (£)	Annual Profit (% of capital)
1807		
Lady Juliana	2,004	48
Lord Nelson	1,690	28
Pitt	944	13
Polly	1,003	19
Salus	1,628	35
Surry	1,999	40
1808		
Lady Juliana	1,423	33
Lord Nelson	1,690	28
Pitt	1,673	32
Polly	2,125	40
Salus	1,628	35
Surry	1,627	35
1809		
Lady Juliana	1,410	33
Lord Nelson	1,690	28
Pitt	1,673	32
Polly	2,125	40
Salus	1,628	35
Surry	1,979	42
1810		
Adelphi (1810–11)	251	6
Elizabeth (1810–11)	639	17
Lady Juliana	1,410	33
Lord Nelson	1,690	28
Polly	2,125	40
Salus	1,628	35
Surry	1,336	30
1811		
Europa (1811–12)	404	15
Lady Juliana	1,410	33
Lord Nelson	1,690	28
Polly	2,125	40
Salus	1,628	35
1812		
Cornwall	2,413	39
Lady Juliana	1,738	53
Polly	2,125	40
1813		
Cornwall	879	14

Table O continued

Date	Annual Profit (£)	Annual Profit (% of capital)
Lady Juliana	1,959	35
Lord Nelson (1813–14)	1,566	26
Polly	2,125	40
1814		
Cornwall	2,525	40
Lady Juliana	1,824	44
Lord Nelson	822	13
Polly	2,125	40
1815		
Cornwall	2,990	43
Lady Juliana	1,183	31
Lord Nelson	1,349	25
Polly	2,125	40
1816		
Cornwall	90	1
Lady Juliana	−254	13 loss
Lord Nelson	638	10
Polly	−341	7 loss
1817		
Cornwall	124	2
Lady Juliana	365	14
Lord Nelson	172	3
Polly	250	4
1818		
Cornwall	495	10
Lady Juliana	331	10
Lord Nelson	362	6
Polly	699	9
1819		
Cornwall	317	6
Lady Juliana	−197	8 loss
Lord Nelson	212	3
Polly	432	8
1820		
Cornwall	−298	5 loss
Lady Juliana	425	16
Lord Nelson	−63	1 loss

Table O continued

Date	Annual Profit (£)	Annual Profit (% of capital)
1821		
Cornwall	102	2
Lady Juliana	−183	5 loss
Lord Nelson	89	2
1822		
Cornwall	259	5
Lady Juliana	196	8
Lord Nelson	−30	1 loss
1823		
Cornwall	808	13
Lady Juliana	886	23
Lord Nelson	328	6
1824		
Cornwall	−136	2 loss
Lady Juliana	174	5
1825		
Cornwall	279	5
1826		
Cornwall	−148	3 loss
1828		
Cornwall	−2	0
1829		
Cornwall	28	1

SELECT BIBLIOGRAPHY

Albion, R. G. *Forests and Sea Power. The Timber Problem of the Royal Navy, 1652–1862*, Cambridge, Mass., 1926.

Albion, R. G. 'British shipping and Latin America, 1806–1914', *Journal of Economic History*, XI, 1951.

Anon *The Late Measures of the Shipowners in the Coal Trade*, London, 1786.

Bean, D. *Tyneside*, London, 1971.

Condon, M. E. A. 'The administration of the transport service during the war against revolutionary France, 1793–1802', unpublished Ph.D. thesis, University of London, 1968.

Craig, R. 'The business historian and the shipping industry: a review and prospect', *Business Archives*, XXXIII, 1970.

Craig, R. 'Capital formation in shipping' in J. P. P. Higgins & S. Pollard (eds.), *Aspects of Capital Investment in Great Britain, 1750–1850*, London, 1971.

Craig, R. & Jarvis, R. *Liverpool Registry of Merchant Ships*, Manchester, 1967.

Crouzet, F. (ed.) *Capital Formation in the Industrial Revolution*, London, 1972.

Crouzet, F. 'Wars, blockade and economic change in Europe, 1792–1815', *Journal of Economic History*, XXIV, 1964.

Crowhurst, P. *The Defence of British Trade, 1689–1815*, Folkestone, 1977.

Davis, R. 'Maritime history: progress and problems', in S. Marriner (ed.), *Business and Businessmen*, Liverpool, 1978.

Davis, R. *The Rise of the English Shipping Industry in the Seventeenth and Eighteenth Centuries*, London, 1962.

Dougan, D. *The History of North-East Shipbuilding*, London, 1968.

Dunn, M. *An Historical, Geological and Descriptive View of the Coal Trade of the North of England*, Newcastle, 1844.

Edington, R. *A Treatise on the Coal Trade*, London, 1813.

Emsley, C. 'The recruitment of petty offenders during the French wars, 1793–1815', *Mariner's Mirror*, LXVI, 1980.

Finch, R. *Coals from Newcastle*, Lavenham, 1973.

Garstin, C. (ed.) *Samuel Kelly*, London, 1925.

Goldenberg, J. A. 'An analysis of shipbuilding sites in Lloyd's Register of 1776', *Mariner's Mirror*, LIX, 1973.

Harris, J. R. 'Copper and shipping in the eighteenth century', *Economic History Review*, 2nd ser., XIX, 1966–7.

Hausman, W. J. *Public Policy and the Supply of Coal to London, 1700–70*, Urbana, Illinois, 1981.

Hausman, W. J. 'Size and profitability of English colliers in the eighteenth century', *Business History Review*, LI, 1977.

Hueckel, G. 'War and the British economy, 1793–1815: a general equilibrium analysis', *Explorations in Economic History*, X, 1972.

Humble, A. F. 'An old Whitby collier', *Mariner's Mirror*, LXI, 1975.

Imlah, A. *Economic Elements in the Pax Britannica*, Cambridge, Mass., 1958.

Jackson, G. *British Whaling Trade*, London, 1978.

Jackson, G. *Hull in the Eighteenth Century*, London, 1972.

Jackson, G. *Trade and Shipping of Eighteenth-Century Hull*, York, 1975.

Jarvis, R. 'Eighteenth century London shipping' in A. Hollaender & W. Kellaway (eds.), *Studies in London History*, London, 1969.

Jones, S. 'Community and organisation: early seamen's trade unionism on the north-east coast, 1768–1844', *Maritime History*, III, 1973.

Jones, S. 'A maritime history of the port of Whitby, 1700–1914', unpublished Ph.D. thesis, University of London, 1972.

Kenwood, A. G. 'Port investment in England and Wales, 1851–1913', *Yorkshire Bulletin of Economic and Social Research*, XVII, 1965.

Lloyd, C. *The British Seaman*, London, 1968.

McCord, N. 'The impress service in north-east England during the Napoleonic wars', *Mariner's Mirror*, 54, 1968.

McCord, N. 'The seamen's strike of 1815 in north-east England', *Economic History Review*, 2nd ser., XXI, 1968.

McCord, N. 'Tyneside discontents and Peterloo', *Northern History*, II, 1967.

MacGregor, D. *The Merchant Sailing Ship, 1775–1815*, London, 1985.

MacPherson, D. *Annals of Commerce*, London, 1805.

Naish, G. 'Shipbuilding' in C. Singer (ed.), *History of Technology*, Oxford, 1958.

North, D. C. 'Ocean freight rates and economic development, 1750–1913', *Journal of Economic History*, XVIII, 1958.

North, D. C. 'Sources of productivity change in ocean shipping, 1600–1850', *Journal of Political Economy*, LXXVI, 1968.

Palmer, S. & Williams, G. (eds.) *Charted and Uncharted Waters*, London, 1982.

Palmer, S. 'The character and organisation of the shipping industry of the port of London, 1815–49', unpublished Ph.D. thesis, University of London, 1979.

Pares, R. *A West India Fortune*, London, 1950.

Parkinson, C.N. (ed.) *Trade Winds*, London, 1948.

Payne, P. *British Entrepreneurship in the Nineteenth Century*, London, 1974.

Pollard, S. *The Genesis of Modern Management*, London, 1965.

Potter, J. 'The British timber duties', *Economica*, new ser., XXII, 1955.

Press, J. 'The economic and social conditions of the merchant seamen of England, 1815–54', unpublished Ph.D. thesis, University of Bristol, 1978.

Rowe, D.J. 'The decline of the Tyneside keelmen in the nineteenth century', *Northern History*, IV, 1969.

Smith, R.B. *Sea Coal for London*, London, 1961.

Stern, W.M. 'The first London dock boom and the growth of the West India docks', *Economica*, new ser., XIX, 1952.

Stevenson, J. *Observations on the Coal Trade in the port of Newcastle upon-Tyne*, Newcastle, 1789.

Sweezy, P.M. *Monopoly and Competition in the English Coal Trade, 1550–1850*, Cambridge, Mass., 1938.

Syrett, D. *Shipping and the American War, 1775–83*, London, 1970.

Syrett, D. 'The organisation of British trade convoys during the American war, 1775–83', *Mariner's Mirror*, LXII, 1976.

Thomas, E.G. 'The old Poor Law and maritime apprenticeship', *Mariner's Mirror*, LXIII, 1977.

Ville, S. 'The deployment of English merchant shipping, 1770–1830: the example of Michael and Joseph Henley', *Journal of Transport History*, 3rd ser., V, 1984.

Ville, S. 'James Kirton, shipping agent', *Mariner's Mirror*, LXVII, 1981.

Ville, S. 'Michael Henley and Son, London shipowners, 1775–1830; with special reference to the war experience', unpublished Ph.D. thesis, University of London, 1984.

Ville, S. 'Size and profitability of English colliers in the eighteenth century: a reappraisal', *Business History Review*, LVIII, 1984.

Ville, S. 'Wages, prices and profitability in the shipping industry during the Napoleonic wars', *Journal of Transport History*, 3rd ser., II, 1981.

Wiener, M. *English Culture and the Decline of the Industrial Spirit, 1850–1980*, Cambridge, 1981.

Williams, D. 'Bulk carriers and timber imports: the British North American trade and the shipping boom of 1824–5', *Mariner's Mirror*, 54, 1968.

Winter, J.M. (ed.) *War and Economic Development*, Cambridge, 1975.

Wright, C. & Fayle, C. *A History of Lloyd's*, London, 1928.

INDEX